FENCING

The Skills of the Game

FENCING

The Skills of the Game

HENRY DE SILVA

THE CROWOOD PRESS

*First published in 1991 by
The Crowood Press Ltd
Ramsbury, Marlborough
Wiltshire SN8 2HR*

Paperback edition 1997

This impression 1999

British Library Cataloguing in Publication Data

A catalogue record for this book is available from the British Library.

ISBN 1 86126 068 7

Acknowledgements

*Front cover photograph courtesy of Action Plus
Back cover photograph by Graham Morrison*

*Line illustrations by Steven Derry
Text photographs by Mr B. Cox*

*I would like to thank: Lt. Clarke and Lt.-Com. Cooke, RN, who started
me off fencing; Peter Lennon, Geoff Hawkesworth, John Fairhall
and Bob Anderson who moulded my progress both as a fencer
and as a coach; Mrs. P. D. Silva who typed my notes; my staff
room who helped with the grammar; Steve Wright who lent
his body for the text photos; and John McGrath, RN for his
history of fencing.*

*Throughout this book, the pronouns 'he', 'him' and 'his' have been
used inclusively and are intended to apply to both men and women.*

*Typeset by Alacrity Phototypsesetters
Banwell Castle, Weston-super-Mare.
Printed and bound in Great Britain by WBC Book Manufacturers Ltd*

Contents

Henry de Silva started fencing in 1947 at the age of fourteen. He has won medals with all weapons, his best result being a gold in the Ontario Open Épée. He has coached fencing for over thirty years and continues to do so today for the Royal Navy, schools and veterans. He is a lecturer in physical education at Charles Keene College.

Henry de Silva is one of those masters of fencing without whom British fencing would never have survived nor many of its achievements been made. Never a man to compromise his beliefs, Henry has fought long and hard with many adversaries, both on and off the piste. He very seldom loses. I have crossed swords with Henry on many levels, always enjoyed the battle, sometimes won, sometimes lost; but it has always been without rancour.

The book he has written is one of the most comprehensive manuals on fencing that I have read. There is not an aspect of the game, including equipment, that he has not covered. What is particularly intriguing is the way he can put a common touch to his subject. Many fencing text books suffer from being so technical that they become boring; not so *Fencing: The Skills of the Game*

Raymond Paul
British Olympic Team
1952, 1956

Olympic Finalist

Four Times National Foil Champion

Empire and Commonwealth
Gold Medal Foil

Henry de Silva has been coaching fencing for over thirty years. As well as being a coach, he is still an active fencer himself. He has founded the National Veterans Fencing Association and he is a full member of the British Institute of Sports Coaches. His sport has taken him round the world, and the wealth of experience and expertise he has accumulated is reflected in his new book. History, equipment, skills and techniques are covered in detail and there are some absorbing issues raised in other chapters.

Fencing: The Skills of the Game, is comprehensive in its coverage of the sport and will provide something of interest for all grades of performer and coach from beginner to expert, and is sure to fill a gap on the sporting bookshelves.

Geoff Cooke
Chief Executive
The British Institute of Sports Coaches

Introduction

Fencing needs a great deal of athleticism and self-control, and requires high levels of individual skill, tactical awareness and mental and physical fitness. Coaches and fencers must put in many hours of hard work to prepare and meet the demands of modern-day tournaments.

There is a large gap between top European and top British fencers at the grass roots level in schools and clubs. However, the performance of top-class fencers should act as a mirror to other aspiring champions.

The international fencer's method of performing his skills has been based on a good solid foundation: although a house may have a firm foundation, what is built above this foundation may vary and can reflect both good and bad workmanship. The coach must therefore lay firm foundations to develop accomplished fencers. A less experienced coach can lay bad habits.

The problem many coaches face is keeping up with developments in the sport. Many coaches are no longer active and rely on what they learnt many years before. There have been many changes – in the rules, the number of competitions and the awareness of fitness and nutrition. Coaches are also now realizing that sports psychology is of great importance and so the language of the sport has changed. If coaches are not fully aware of developments, it may eventually be detrimental to youngsters' progress, resulting in them having to try to unlearn bad habits which, as most people know, is very difficult. The grip is a good example of this. Often the student's index finger does not grip the foil handle correctly and the thumb is not flat, but pinching the handle. It must be stressed that many fencing skills are difficult to master and the pupil's progress is only gradual.

This book is all about skills, and these must form the chief part of the sport. Tactical moves break down because of skill failure on the piste and coaches must be able to diagnose these errors, treat the problem and hope there is a cure, the result of which should be a better performance. Some problems may be small, while others may need a complete transplant. Some faults cannot be cured and so other methods to bypass the fault must be put into operation to get the required result. The coach must understand the technique used and its application in great detail and must ensure that practices are realistic and relevant for all levels and are related to fight situations.

HISTORY OF FENCING

Fencing and swordsmanship today are synonymous, but in the past swordsmanship was just a part of fencing; you only have to look through old books to see a splendid array of weapons.

'Foil' is the most characteristic word in the fencing vocabulary, but has no proven derivation. The best guess by *The Oxford English Dictionary*, 'from failed or blunted weapon', embraces all three of the modern fencing weapons: foil, épée and sabre.

The earliest recorded fencing match took place at The Temple of Madinet Habu, erected by Rameses III in about 1190BC, near Luxor. Weapons had points and guards

1

then, but the non sword-arm was used to protect the face. The Romans had gladiatorial schools, but the Greeks preferred boxing.

Medieval Fencing

The medieval version of hooliganism gave fencing a bad name during this period. As a result, fencing tuition within the City of London was banned by Edward I in 1285. This ban remained effective for over 400 years. The government of that time considered fencing masters to be the equivalent of vagrants, but retained them for the principals in the 'Trials of Combat'. This had its risks, because it was found that a master had bet against his pupil and had won and profited from this, penalties were harsh. For example, Elias Pugin in 1220 was sentenced to lose a foot and fist. His appeal was upheld and he lost his foot only and was told to be grateful for such leniency.

Age of the Rapier

In the sixteenth century the sword evolved into the rapier, a weapon over 1 m (1 yd) long and weighing about a kilogram (2.2 lb). It was the Italian School of Fencing which dominated Europe until the mid-seventeenth century. Positions in those days were not guards, for the non sword-arm, whether mailed, shielded, or holding another short sword was used for defence. It is also noticeable that the opposite foot to the sword-arm was advanced. Soon it was realized that if the sword-arm itself was advanced, you could develop a lunge. By 1610 it was becoming clear that a thrust was faster and the resulting injury more serious.

In 1599, an amateur coach, George Silver, tried to prove that a cut with a curved sword was faster than a direct thrust. These foils, of which few survive (now in the Victoria and Albert Museum, London), were formidable. Averie Borwick, a yeoman, was killed in practice at a fencing school in the same year.

The Spanish Style

The Spanish style was different from the rest of Europe. Thibault of 1628 related the nature of footwork to a dance executed on the tangents and chords of a circle drawn using the rapier blade as its radius.

The second difference was the very upright stance with the rigid sword-arm holding the blade as a threat to face or body, but it still produced swordsmen whose exceptional strength and stamina were universally respected.

The English Scene

There is plenty of evidence to show that many in this country preferred the robust swordsmanship of the heavy, cutting broadswords to the more technical skills of rapier fencing. Henry VIII, a great enthusiast for combat sports, granted patent to the Masters of Defence who qualified for the privilege of teaching sportsmanship by giving public demonstrations, known as prizes, of their proficiency with an impressive array of weapons. *Paradoxes of Defence* by George Silver, 1599, is the only known book on their methods. The only main source of the merits of sword-play was to be found in plays, and by the middle of the seventeenth century, these had degenerated into blood-letting for the benefit of the audience.

French Influence

At the court of Louis XIV a lighter weapon known as the small sword evolved and with it emerged the dominance of French fencing.

At the same time the foil was developed as a light practice weapon. Although the

Development of Fencing

1190 BC	Rameses III. Probably used short swords (combat)
1285	Edward I bans fencing in London
16th C.	Development of rapier
1536	Marozzo publishes first popular fencing book
1540	Henry VIII grants patents to fencing masters
1599	Averie Borwick killed in practice at a fencing school
1628	Thibault relates footwork to a dance round a circle and publishes book on Spanish school
18th C.	Angelo family dominates fencing in England up until just before 1900
1780	Invention of wire mask
19th C.	The Services organize fencing in England
1886	First demonstration of electric fencing by Mr Little
1933	First electric World Épée Championship
1936	Electric fencing at Berlin Olympics
1950s	Bob Anderson develops National Training Scheme
1955	First Electric World Foil Championship
1956	Gillian Sheen wins Olympic Gold
1986	First electric World Sabre Championship

button was wrapped in leather to the size of a musket ball, there was danger of getting one in the eye.

Disarming was still taught. Blood gladiatorial contests were well advertised in the press. Fogg, in a career of 271 fights, lost only once. Masters, such as Liancour, were encouraging the practice of fighting along an imaginary straight line as used today, instead of traversing from side to side as in rapier fighting. The lunge was now universally accepted as the most efficient method of attack and the use of the left hand had declined as a means of protecting the face.

Eighteenth-Century Fencing

Fencing in England was dominated by the Angelo family from Italy from the 1750s to nearly 1900.

Angelo illustrations command high prices.

Some were drawn by John Gerwyn, a founder member of the Royal Academy and some were engraved by Ryland, who was later hanged for forgery.

During this period many of today's conventions of foil play were instigated, for example having only the trunk as the valid target, and following the strict sequence of attack, parry, riposte. There was also a convention, now not used, when no riposte was made until the attacker had recovered to the on guard position. These rules were brought in for reasons of safety and to reduce blinding. 'One in the eye' could be an inspired phrase in the English language.

These rules initiated a period of stagnation of fencing through lack of mobility. The left hand was still used occasionally for parrying and disarming, and also to guard against foul play.

1780 saw the invention of the wire mask by

La Boissière. Why so late an obvious invention? Perhaps because wire mesh had not been developed until then. This invention still did not improve the mobility of the fencers through increased safety. Domenico Angelo provided training aids especially for use by drill instructors and was appointed Cutlass Instructor for the Navy.

The Revival

It took a generation for professional teachers to realize that the mask presented an opportunity to exploit the demand for speed and mobility as well as grace and accuracy of movement. Masters like Jean-Louis and Bertrand in the first half of the nineteenth century realized the mask presented an opportunity to exploit the demand for speed and mobility as well as grace and accuracy of movement. Masters also realized that the lightweight foil could be manipulated with the fingers more accurately than with the wrist, and this led to an economy of effort, which is still characteristic of good fencing.

Épée and Sabre

As a reaction against the conventions of foil, a group of French fencers in the second half of the nineteenth century demanded practice with the duelling épée. This brought about some basic principles: for instance, the whole body became the legitimate target. At the same time the Italian master Radaelis developed the light fencing sabre.

The final organization of fencing from club to international standard was taken up by the Services. Many years before the National Championships were held in the early twentieth century, the Services organized fencing competition at the Royal Tournament, first with foil, eleven years later with sabre and, in 1901, with the épée.

The Present Century

The most significant change has been the advent of electric apparatus, and although a demonstration was held on 24 June 1886 by a Mr Little, development was slow and it was not until 1933 that it gained official recognition at épée competitions. The first public demonstration was at the Berlin Olympics in 1936. With the foil, there was a problem in that they had not yet devised a system which would differentiate between on and off targets. In 1955 this problem was solved and the sabre was also introduced to the system in 1986.

Increase in gamesmanship has led to a whole new category of penalty hits. However, fencing should be a conversation of the sword; an artistic co-ordination of movement by body and blade.

1 Basics

PRESENTATION

How material is presented in skill-learning situations is critical. The coach's ability to demonstrate each technique is of the utmost importance. If a demonstration is good and practices well structured, it might not be necessary to give too much information at once. For example, I once asked a group to extend their arms to match mine. I was criticizing them for not extending fully when a pupil pointed out to me that mine was not extended fully either, albeit due to a permanently broken arm.

In some sports, it is the depth of knowledge of the coach that produces the champions. One gymnastic coach was riddled with arthritis, but produced an Olympic gymnast. The coach not only has to overcome his limitations, but to overcome the problems of his pupils. While the extent of the coach's knowledge has to be considerable, the amount of information given to an individual must be the minimum necessary to cure a fault.

Well-structured practices will enable the fencer to progress at his own level in a logical way. As all individuals are different, pupils will progress at different rates and should be allowed to progress at their own speed in order to realize their full potential.

SCHOOLS AND CLUBS

Many factors have led to a downward trend in developments in schools. There are fewer training colleges with fencing clubs; fewer people from the Services with knowledge of fencing; and as fencing is a minority sport there is little or no funding from the education authorities, therefore, headmasters will not lay out for expensive equipment.

Fencing is not part of a PE programme. Because many teachers do not run out-of-school activities, clubs have benefitted by an increase of young members. (Many children love seeing sword-fights on television and films and play sword-fighting with their friends.) However, there is little opportunity for most to develop a serious liking for fencing as there are so few fencing clubs and of those, few that cater for children; any other classes are usually held too late for them to stay up for and lastly, adults do not like working with children. Competition is also an essential part of a child's make-up, but this should only be carefully introduced, once the basic skills have been grasped.

BASIC LANGUAGE

The age at which youngsters are introduced to fencing varies in different parts of the world. I would recommend starting at eight years old, but some seven year olds are big and strong enough. It is difficult, if not impossible, to say what should be taught at any age. The Russians give youngsters specific tests in flexibility, fitness, co-ordination, aggressiveness and mental aptitude. If they do not succeed, they are encouraged to try another sport.

The four stages in the learning process:

Basics

1. The beginner
2. The developer
3. The improving fencer
4. The advanced fencer

The period of time of each stage depends on the ability of the fencer to assimilate knowledge and transfer this into a quality performance based on the quality of coaching and guidance the individual receives.

Only a certain number are going to be Internationals and a few Olympic stars, so basic skills must be taught correctly at first. Some might not reach beyond the first stage, but should still enjoy their game through acquiring a sound basic language.

The beginner must develop a feel for the right weapon. Children can now get size 2 and size 3 foils, which are much lighter and easier to manipulate. The coach should get pupils to work together in pairs. He should set them a specific task and should reassess each lesson – he may have to adapt during a particular lesson either to a group or to an individual.

When I first started fencing, it was six months before I was allowed to cross swords. The pendulum has swung the other way and there is too much free play because coaches do not have a structured programme. When the pupil has a sound basic foundation, he can be introduced to a minor competition and encouraged to play against good players.

EQUIPMENT

Shoes

Shoes should be comfortable and roomy, as feet swell after a lot of activity. When choosing your shoe, it is important to ensure that the width is correct. The width of your hand is

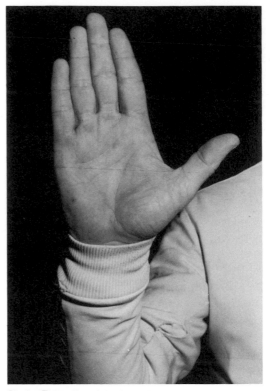

Fig 1 The palm of the hand is the same width as the foot.

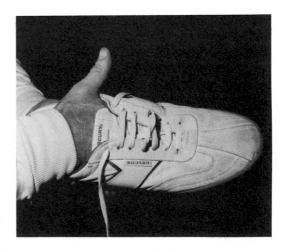

Fig 2 Palm fits into shoe, showing correct width.

the same as your foot and so if your hand lays flat inside the shoe, it should be the correct width for your foot. The shoe should be flexible: you should be able to bend the toe to the heel. The back of the shoe should be firm and not bend over.

It is best to take both a leather-soled shoe and a rubber one to competitions since it is not always possible to know in advance the surface of the piste.

Clothing

Fencing can be considered to be one of the safest sports because of the amount of protective clothing used. Patched and worn clothing should not be worn. Care should be taken in washing and the instructions on the label followed. Clothing should be hung and dried after use.

Clothing should allow free movement, especially under the armpits and also in the legs.

Jacket

The jacket should be of cotton and zip up at the rear. Ladies' jackets allow breast protectors to be added. When buying, make sure that the jacket is loose under the armpits, across the back, and long enough in the arms and body.

Breeches

Breeches should fasten below the knees and on the opposite side to the fencing arm. They should also be loose in the legs so that they allow the fencer unrestricted movement when lunging.

Gloves

Gloves should be of soft white leather and have light foam padding. It is important to try gloves on before buying.

Masks

Masks are very important. They should be comfortable and not wobble on the head. Care should be taken of the mesh and it should be examined regularly, especially if someone hits it hard. It should not be left with sweaty clothing in case it goes rusty. One should never lend one's mask to another fencer. Everyone's head is a different shape and it puts a strain on the backpiece, which can break (although backpieces that are elastic are less vulnerable). The bib of the mask should be firmly attached and checked regularly. Leon Paul masks are marked with a blob of metal on the top denoting small; a letter M denoting medium (or no indication), a single disc denoting large and two discs for extra large.

Foil

You will need a non-electric ordinary French-handled sword, size 3 for under-14s, size 5 for over-14s. Paul Etoile is a satisfactory blade for beginners.

The cost of a foil is less than most other sports' main equipment, but before you buy any equipment, discuss your individual requirements with your fencing coach who will be able to advise you. The majority of sports shops have no idea of what is what.

Maintenance of Blades and Masks

Blades should have a slick of oil applied, and then be wiped clean before use. They should be lightly burnished so as to get rid of rough edges. Guards should be inspected for rust and bent guards should be reshaped.

Basics

Blades are pre-tempered by the manufacturers and, if used correctly, will last a long time. Rough play or full lunges at close quarters will result in badly bent blades. A blade kinked in the opposite way to the natural bend should be discarded, as it is dangerous. If you get a large bend the other way, lay the foil on the floor and draw your foot several times along the blade, then use your hands to straighten it. If you draw the blade at an angle it could break.

Maintenance of masks includes regular checks to see that the mesh is not damaged. After use, they should be wiped dry as breath condenses on the wire, as does perspiration. The stitching in mask and clothing should also be checked regularly and any necessary repair undertaken by a professional.

Instructions for Rewiring Electric Foils

1. Remove blade from weapon.
2. Remove retaining grub screws, also tension spring and tip; clean tip with cleaning fluid.
3. Remove wire from blade (it might need to be prised out), a Stanley blade will do the trick. Break the wire at base point.
4. Remove the wire contacts inside the base by pushing a paper clip or similar wire into the base from the blade.
5. Clean blade thoroughly. Remove all traces of the old resin.
6. With the groove in the blade uppermost, bend the tang downwards so that the end of the tang is 2½cm (1in) out of line with the blade. Also bend the blade downwards about 6cm (2⅜in) from the shoulder. This ensures that the blade wire will sit down at the shoulder where the blade groove is shallow. Wind some tape around the middle of the tang.
7. Insert the blade wire into the point base, lay in the groove and pull taut. Apply the resin. Allow to dry for twenty-four hours. To ensure that the wire sets in the groove, bow the blade to the extent of a normal kit and allow to set in that position. When dry, unwind the wire from the tang, remove the tape and mount the blade.
8. Assemble the point.

Information from
Leon Paul Equipment Company Limited

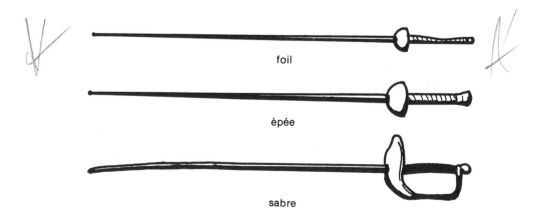

foil

épée

sabre

Fig 3   Weapons used in fencing.

CHOICE OF WEAPON

There are three main weapons: foil, épée and sabre. Foil fencing is the basis of all modern fencing. Masters abroad will encourage pupils to pick up one weapon and one weapon only, but in Britain, pupils tend to have a go at all three.

The development of the foil has been largely influenced by the Italian and French schools. In the eighteenth century, the rapier was too heavy and cumbersome to wear in society. The court sword developed blade was shortened and the hilt was smaller.

The lighter weapon had to be used with considerable skill and precision. Fencing can, from gymnastic exercises, become graceful accomplishment. Stress was placed more on shortness and speed of movement than on strength; and the manipulators, that is thumb and first finger, were emphasized. A famous maxim attributed to the French master Jean-Louis and in the film *Scaramouche*: 'A foil should be held as one holds a bird; not so tightly as to crush it, but just enough to prevent it escaping from the hand.'

When the duel declined and fencing came to be regarded as a sport, both the French and Italians developed their foil play. The

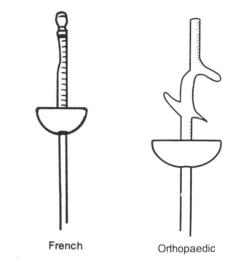

French   Orthopaedic

Fig 4 Style of grips.

Italians retained the quillons within the guard while the French relied on finger-work.

The French foil is the most subtle, and in speed of blade-work excels, owing to the free play allowed to the fingers. Today, we have the orthopaedic-aid pistol grip, but my preference for beginners is to practise with the French grip and work on the dexterity of the fingers.

The foil is split into portions (*see* Fig 5). There are two main sizes of foil: a size 5 for

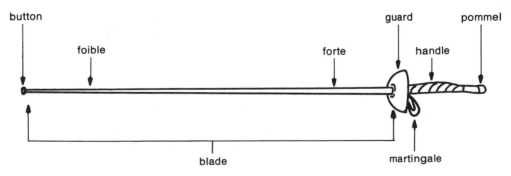

button   foible   forte   guard   handle   pommel

blade   martingale

Fig 5 Parts of a foil.

adults and a size 3 for youngsters, much lighter than the adult's blade. Before use, especially in cold weather, rub the blade on the sole of your shoe several times. This causes friction and warms the blade. This technique is also useful when you have hit your opponent awkwardly and caused the blade to bend the wrong way. Never stand on the end and hope to straighten it — it will snap. The reason for warming the blade is that when metal is cold it is brittle and a broken blade in competition can be dangerous.

Your own personal foil is the weapon you will use in practise and to win fights and you should get used to the feel and the balance of it. Several times, I have blindfolded a pupil, put his sword amongst others, and every time he has picked out his own. So it is essential that you should have your own as soon as possible.

When you buy a foil, press the point to the floor, bending the blade. On release it should straighten. If it does not, or if the blade bends with difficulty, do not buy it. Choose one that feels comfortable in your hand.

To test the equilibrium of the foil, place the forefinger of the hand along the blade about an inch from the guard. The foil should be equally balanced in order to project the point to the target.

The maximum length of blade from guard to point is less than 90 cm (35⅜ in), maximum diameter of the guard is 12.25 cm (4¾ in). The maximum weight is under 500 g (17⅝ oz). It is best to have a lighter blade. The total length of hilt from inside of guard to pommel is 23 cm (9⅛ in).

Quite often, when buying a foil, the tang is straight and with the handle on it does not feel comfortable in the hand. Ask your coach to set it for you: he will slightly bend the handle down and to the left (if you are right-handed).

Fencers use pistol grips to withstand stronger beats and parries. They give a stronger grip and are used by fencers for tough fighting, but these grips do hinder the use of thumb and forefinger. Foil play will lay the foundation of style and style is of importance for success in sport.

THE GRIP

The manner in which the foil is held is all-important. With the French handle (as shown in Fig 4) the ferrule should be towards the guard, arching upwards and curved to the right. Place the handle on the second joint of the index finger, and grip firmly, placing the thumb on top of the wide face.

Lay the other three fingers along the handle so that the fingertips lay alongside the narrow left-hand edge. Make sure that the thumb and index finger are against the pad. (Some try to hold the handle by the pommel, supposedly to gain length, but a strong beat will deflect the blade and leave the target open.) Do not pinch or nip the handle. When properly gripped, the pommel is close to, but not resting on, the wrist.

When you are more experienced, turn to one o'clock with the thumb on top; the

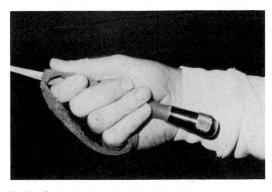

Fig 6   Correct grip: aids along handle.

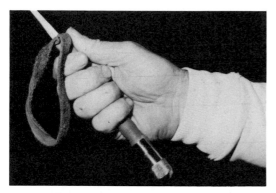

Fig 7   The grip showing pommel not in wrist and the aids gripping the handle, making the thumb appear pinched.

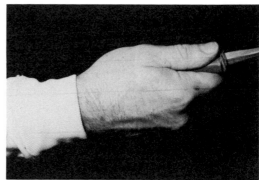

Fig 8   Hand in supination.

Fig 9   Correct grip and angle of sword to elbow: a straight line; foil in half-supination.

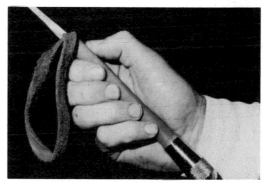

Fig 10   Thumb and finger pads pinching the handle.

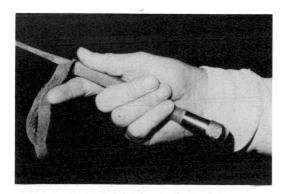

Fig 11   Index finger elongated, not gripping the handle.

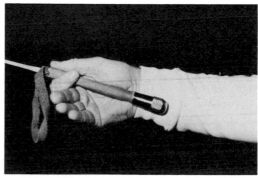

Fig 12   The grip showing the pommel in wrist.

fingers are on the side, the foil is in half superation.

The other positions can be mentioned. Pronation, knuckles on top; and supination, fingers on top.

The thumb and index finger, that is the manipulators, not the wrist, control the blade. They control lateral, circular and semi-circular movements. The other fingers are relaxed and are called aids. They give assistance by opening and closing the handle.

There should be no gap between the thumb and handle. Many people bend the hand so there is a rounded curve between hand and wrist. This strains the tendon, causing tiredness, and keeps the blade too low to be manipulated. Look at the base of the thumb – if gripped properly there should be a hollow.

SKILL

The Target

The characteristics of fencing at foil are: the restriction of the target to the trunk of the body; the timing of the hit; and the distance from the target when the hit is made.

Most books show the torso cut into four: sixte, quarte, octave, septime (or high inside, high outside, low inside, low outside). I do not agree with this conventional description of the target because if you are on guard in sixte and asked to parry quarte, you do not go through sixte in order to get to quarte. If you have a position of central guard, yes. Quarte is left of your blade when you are on guard in sixte and, conversely, sixte is

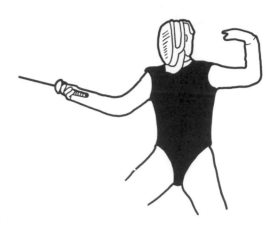

Fig 13   The foil target.

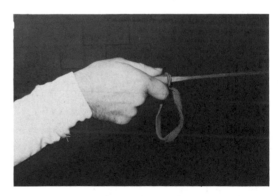

Fig 14   Wrong grip: wrist bent, therefore no straight line from point to elbow; no extension of the fingers.

everything right of your blade when you are on guard in quarte. This also relates to octave and septime and also applies to the position of your hand, either high or low. If you hold your hand high, everything beneath is low; if your hand is low, everything above is high.

2 Skills

Skills cover a wide range of sensory and motor activity called motor skills. Motor skills, which coaches are mainly concerned with in levels of performance, are manipulative, overall body skills, co-ordination, flexibility and reaction skills, including perception. Skill must develop in a sensible order and should have an end result. It is achieved with repetitive practice.

Fencing skills require sensory input (stimulus):

Processing of information received.

Output (response) movement.
Constant feedback and evaluation.

ON GUARD

This is the position from which you can either attack or defend. It is a balanced position. One should be able to pick the feet up and put them down without moving the centre of gravity.

First, stand upright and place the feet at right angles (heel to heel); move the right

Fig 15   Ladies' foil. Good attack by fencer on left, but poor hand control, therefore missing.

13

Skills

Fig 16 Ladies' foil. Fencer on left is in a poorly balanced position, therefore missing. Fencer on right needs only to place her point, blade bent upwards showing that one arm has been used instead of fingers when fixing.

elbow. The classical style for your back arm is held there for several reasons:

1. It opens the rib cage, giving you greater breathing capacity.
2. It keeps the arm out of the way, the ruling being that if any of the rear arm covers the target, the fencer will incur a warning, which, if repeated, will result in a hit being awarded against him for that bout only.
3. It reduces the size of the target by keeping the left shoulder well back.
4. Like the rudder of a ship, it balances and guides the body when making the lunge and prevents the body from falling forward when making the lunge. Falling over with a mask on is particularly painful.

heel forward the length of your right foot, to where the toe was then move it again to where the top shoe lace was. (The distance between your two heels should now be approximately 1⅔ the length of your foot.) This I have found suitable for fencers since the taller the person, the larger his feet. Therefore, his stance will need to be wider than that of a smaller person.

Now bend the knees. From this position, you should just be able to see your toe in front of the knee. Next, place your hips to the front, body upright, rear arm raised, elbow just above the level of the shoulder, sword-arm extended so that elbow is one hand span from body, forearm at the horizontal and head looking straight ahead. The point of the foil overlooking your opponent's left shoulder should be in a straight line with your

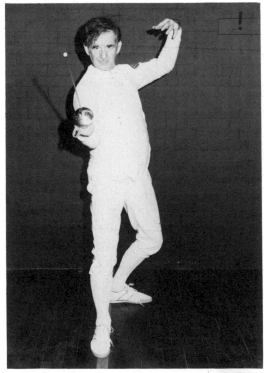

Fig 17 On guard from the front in sixte; point at shoulder level.

Fig 18   *Correct on guard position.*

Fig 19   *On guard. Elbow is hand's span from the body.*

Fig 20   *The position of the foil shows that the weight is evenly distributed.*

Fig 21   *On guard position. The position of the foil shows that the fencer's weight is leaning forward.*

Fig 22 *On guard position viewed from the rear. Note the angle of the rear knee.*

MOVEMENT

First try and pick your feet up without swaying the body backwards and forwards. Next, start moving forward and back, still high stepping, keeping small steps. Big steps lose time and also give a false awareness of distance; and they also affect judgement. Try moving backwards and forwards like an Eastern dancer, as on a cushion of air.

When performing these exercises or training skills, beginners should have frequent breaks as antagonistic muscles soon get tired.

To learn the step forward, first place the toe of the right foot on a line, then move the foot forward to place the heel on the line (so that you have moved forward one length of your foot). To make it clearer, lift the front toe, move the foot across the floor, place the heel down and smartly bring the rear foot forward, at the same time as the front toe comes down. This means that the step forward is

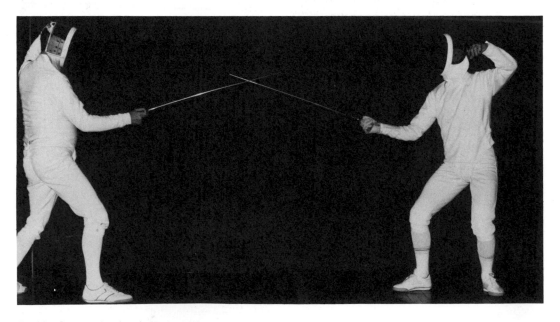

Fig 23 *On guard at fencing measure.*

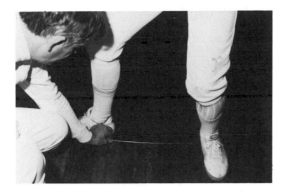

Fig 24   *Method of checking and maintaining distance between the feet by measuring with the foil.*

Fig 25   *Arm extended. Parry in sixte.*

Fig 26   *Extension with front foot moving forward.*

one movement and not, as is often practised, two movements. When practising the step, keep the rear leg bent, which will prevent it from being brought too near the front foot.

The best exponent of mobility and the lunge was John Feathers, the Australian National Coach.

Practice

For the following exercise, pupils should be in pairs, one with and one without a foil. The pupil without a foil stands on guard with the feet the correct distance apart. The pupil with the foil places the point against one heel and holds the foil against the other heel. He keeps hold of the foil and then asks the other person to move forward and backward, then stop. Check the gap between the heels and adjust. It is surprising how pupils get to know their distance this way. Pupils can also lunge and recover and check the distance.

When moving, the body should not bob up and down. If you have a gym beam, lower it to the on guard height and move forward and back beneath it. This will prevent any bobbing. If a beam is not available, a long bamboo cane held over the fencer's head by the coach will achieve the same effect.

The advance followed immediately by the lunge is known as an attack by en marchant. It is useful for both simple and complex movements and develops a sense of time. Scientifically, it is better because when attacking from a straight lunge, you have to overcome initial inertia, but preceded by a step forward more power can be executed in the lunge.

THE LUNGE

The lunge is the basis of attack, the method of delivering the body towards your opponent

Fig 27   The lunge.

Fig 28   The on guard position showing the line of centre of gravity.

at a practical distance so that you are able to hit your opponent with sufficient force. It is learned early and is practised continually. The lunge is in two parts: first, the development; second, the return or recovery. Try and think of it as one unbroken movement and remember that it has not been fully executed until the return to the on guard position.

Development

First, extend the arm, not from the shoulder, but from the manipulators. The extension can be compared to stretching a piece of elastic. If you jerk your arm out, you contract the muscle fibres, thereby shortening the extension. Jerk the arm out and check the distance. Next, stretch the arm out from the manipulators. You will notice the difference in distance. When stretching the arm, note that the body does not lean forward.

Next, lift the front toe. Note that the body does not lean back. Thrust from the back leg, projecting the body forward and reserve the final burst of speed for the end.

Distance is important. If you are too close

you will not have reached full speed and if too far away, you have overreached, and speed is reduced as well as power. A simple example is to relate development to the firing of a cannon: the cannon ball is put down the front and rammed down, the fuse is fired from the back depending on the barrel angle, the shot is fired, then there is the recoil.

The right foot should glide forward. Put a coin under the heel and if you are doing it correctly the coin should be pushed along. Too many fencers lunge off their front foot. One way to get a fencer to use the back leg is for the coach to stand behind with a foil in his hand resting just above the fencer's rear knee. As the fencer lunges, the coach should lower the foil. If the foil raps the knee, it shows that the fencer did not push off from his back leg. To begin with, concentrate on smoothness of action rather than speed; speed will follow. It is best to stress at this stage the importance of being relaxed. The lunge is the final movement of the attack and so many fencers tense themselves before launching off. The only tightening should be of the manipulators, but the sword-arm should be flexible and the shoulder well down.

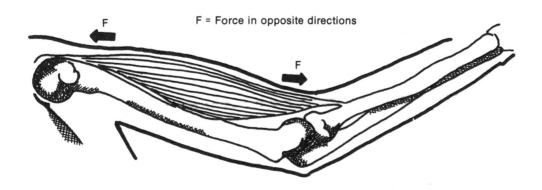

Fig 29 Muscle used in extending the arm.

Recovery

The second part of the lunge should be a well-controlled recovery. When lunging, the heel lands slightly before the rest of the foot moves on to its ball, rebounds back on to the heel, pushes off (at the same time bends the rear leg) and recovers in to the on guard position, bending the sword-arm last.

Practice

In pairs. One fencer on guard, the other with four objects for marking:

1. The fencer lunges. Mark the spot.

2. The fencer does a step and lunges with the front foot only. Mark the spot.
3. The fencer does two steps and lunges with the front foot only. Mark the spot.
4. The fencer lunges. Mark the spot.

Notice that the fourth lunge reaches further than the first because the muscles have been stretched. The coach can influence the distance of the pupil's lunge by altering the tone of his voice: soft, medium soft, loud, very loud.

The rear arm is very important, as it is used as a balance and keeps the body from falling forward. Keep it parallel to the rear leg with fingers outstretched.

Fig 30 Footmarks showing the exercise, how to improve the lunge.

Fig 32　*The lunge correctly executed.*

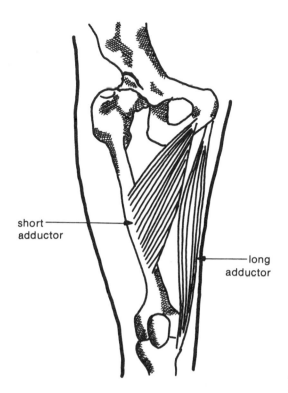

short
adductor

long
adductor

Fig 31　*Muscles used when lunging.*

MORE FOOT MOVEMENTS

L'Appel

This is a sharp rap with the front foot. Imagine the pawing of a horse, where the action is from the knee down. Another method is to hold the foil and place the tip in front of the foot, then kick it. This can be used as a preparation or a diversionary action to distract the opponent from your sword.

Balestra

The balestra is a follow through of l'appel by a jump forward. Lift the front toe, jump forward the same distance as a step forward,

making sure you do not jump upwards and that you are well balanced so that both feet come down together, in order to follow with a lunge. If you are wanting greater distance, bring the rear foot closer to the front foot, then lunge, keeping the rear leg bent so as to get maximum power in the lunge.

Fig 33　*Ladies' foil. Fencer on right is badly balanced, enabling fencer on left to do a successful prime riposte.*

Jump-back (also Balestra)

This is a defensive movement which also can be used as an offensive movement. Jump back and lunge as the opponent moves forward on your jump-back.

The Flèche (Arrow)

Much practice must be put into this movement because once committed, it is impossible to stop. The movement is a sudden surprise attack and, as with all surprise attacks, its use should be limited to when the distance and timing are right, for instance, when the opponent has let slip his concentration.

From the on guard position, lean forward keeping the sword-arm straight. When you feel loss of balance, bring the rear leg through. The front leg now extends vigorously. As the rear leg touches the ground the point should have reached the target. With a flying flèche, the point will have arrived well before both feet touch the floor.

It is important when doing the flèche that you also have strong quadriceps and flexibility in the ankle of the front leg. As the rear leg lands, the weight of the body is transferred forward, releasing the front leg to push vigorously.

Various other steps can be employed, either to close the distance suddenly or just to get out of reach. For a cross-step forward, bring the rear foot in front of the front foot, then bring the front foot forward, finishing in the on guard position. There is also the cross-step backward, and the half cross-step forward which involves taking the rear foot in front of the front foot and then lunging. The half cross-step backward involves bringing the front foot behind the rear foot, then bringing the front foot forward again and lunging. A favourite ploy of mine is to go back two or three paces so that the opponent is really

Fig 34   The flèche. Leaning forward then rear leg carried through.

moving forward, and then to lunge. Balance is essential. Another movement is the back lunge: take the rear leg backwards, finishing in the lunge position.

SIMPLE ATTACKS

Another practice which is useful for dexterity is to stand upright and walk towards your partner with arm straight, disengaging each time as the partner goes from sixte to quarte and so forth, finishing with the hit.

Next, progression: extend the arm and lunge, starting off with one disengage, then two, then more, while your partner does lateral parries.

Disengages need not only be done laterally, but also vertically, going from high to low and low to high. Hitting in the low line requires a different finish, pronation (knuckles on top) on the flank and supination (fingers upright) on the stomach. When your partner does a circular movement, disengage on the final part.

As previously mentioned, you should be loose in the shoulders, arm and fingers, and also alert to the possibilities of attacking. Many fencers tense up before the initial attack, so practise with a partner choosing the opportunity to attack and disengage on the parry. As practice improves, the partner should overload the change of distance, the cadence of his arm and blade movements.

The Cut-Over or French Coupé

This is the action of taking the blade over your opponent's, extending and lunging. It should be used against an opponent who has a low guard. The result is a pressure caused by slightly turning the hand, either to pronation (in quarte) or supination (in sixte)

drawing the wrist back, then hitting. The common fault is drawing the arm back and being hit with a counter-attack. This action loses the fencer the right of way.

From out of distance and absence of blade, the action of waggling the blade with the fingers in front of a person's face can cause that moment of hesitation, either giving you time to deliver the attack or making his counter attack out of time.

The Counter Disengagement

An action by disengagement on a fencer's change of engagement. With a change of engagement fencers will often engage the blade then immediately disengage and engage the blade the other side. This can be done several times, often to see some form of response either by preparing for an attack or provoking an attack. Now comes the counter disengagement. On opponent's change of engagement, for example, when engaging in sixte the opponent disengages and attempts to engage your blade in quarte. You should disengage (follow the other blade) extend and lunge. One very noticeable fault when counter disengaging is to follow the other blade round to touch it before lunging. Counter disengagement can be done in low lines, but is not often used.

DEFENCE

To parry either by quarte or sixte (lateral high parries) or septime or octave (lateral low parries).

Lateral Parry

These are simple or instinctive parries from sixte to quarte. The blade and arm are

Fig 35   Parry quarte.

Fig 36   Parry sixte.

Fig 37   Parry quarte fails because it is made with the middle of the blade and not the forte.

Fig 38   The lunge with parry quarte.

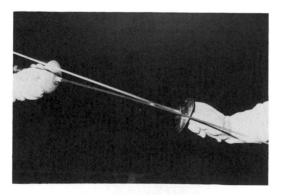

Fig 39   Parry made with the corner of the blade.

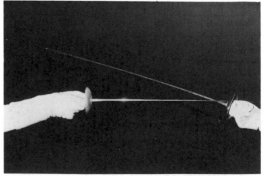

Fig 40   Parry sixte. Point taken too far off target.

Fig 41 An aid to parrying quarte.

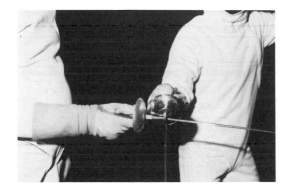

Fig 42 An aid to parrying octave.

carried over in a parallel line from one shoulder to the other, placing the forte of your blade against the blade of your opponent, with the characteristic of deflection, ready for the immediate riposte.

First, without the foil, practise shaking hands; replace the hand with the sword and you will have the right position in quarte. Another practice involves working in groups of three. One lunges, one parries and the other stands at the side with his foil against the defender's coquille (guard). When one fencer lunges, the defender parries while running his guard along the blade of the person at the side. This will ensure that he does not draw his hand back or push it further ahead. This method can also be used in octave and septime.

Circular Parry

From the lateral parry, we can use the circular or counter parry, where the blade scribes a circle coming back to the same spot from where it started. Get a partner to place a finger by the point of the foil when in the on guard position, scribe a circle and the point should come back to the finger. There should be no movement of the hand, in fact

Fig 43 Lunge with parry sixte.

Fig 44 Counter sixte parry. Forte should have been trapping the foible.

Fig 45 Practice for counter sixte. Point too low.

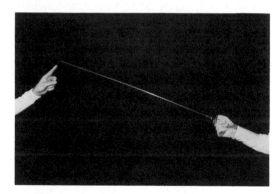

Fig 46 Point too high.

Fig 47 Correct return of point in counter sixte.

with the contraction of the manipulators and a relaxation of the fingers, this can be done easily. Much automatic practice must follow because in a fight, a panic situation will evolve and an easy deception of the blade will follow with no time to make a successive parry.

If you do not make a complete circle, the opposing blade will go through the angle. If you go through more than a circle, the blade will slip under and through.

Some people say you should displace the opponent's point out of line with the target because of the force of the electric blade (which is stronger than a conventional blade), but if the parry is executed correctly and the fingers immediately relaxed, the riposte can be executed quickly and directly without having to direct the 'out-of-line point'.

When parrying, get as much of the forearm behind the hand; when you place the point and extend the muscles, do so in a flowing motion with power. If the upper arm, forearm and hand are flexed in different directions, there is no fluidity in the extension.

We are all told to parry with the forte, but parry with the edge as it is sharper than the flat side. Try it with your finger. When in sixte, have your thumb at one o'clock; when parrying, turn the thumb to eleven o'clock. This will bring the sharp edge to your opponent's blade and will also ensure that the point remains in line. If the point lags behind, the opposing blade can come over the angle and if the point goes too far, the opposing blade goes through the angle beneath. Also, the riposte is delayed.

Semi-Circular Parry

I find these parries are very little practised, as chiefly the arm is used in a wild arc to sweep away the opponent's blade. By using a large movement, it can be deceived by a feint in

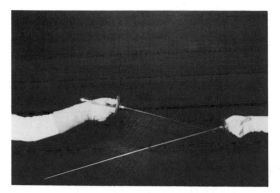

Fig 48   Parry octave; hand not lowered.

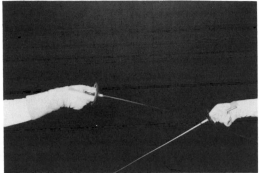

Fig 49   Parry octave; point low.

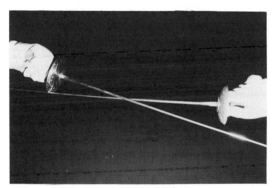

Fig 50   Parry octave. Here showing too much use of wrist.

Fig 51   Parry octave.

Fig 52   A step back after the lunge.

the low line, then coming over the top.

The action spans half a circle, no less and no more. If less, the opposing blade can come through; if more, the opposing blade will come off the top of the guard. Use the manipulators to swing in an inward arc so as to keep the blade out. Leave the point in line with the target and riposte, keeping control of the blade. To riposte high, keep the hand still and use the fingers to place the point. The semi-circular parry can be used in attacks in the high line but the hand needs to be a little higher, therefore making it high septime or high octave.

You can practise doing octave—sixte—octave or septime—quarte—septime against any vertical object. This practice will make sure the blade only goes into the required position. Keep the action of the wrist to a minimum and do not let the elbow swing out.

Octave is useful in that if a person attacks high, the pupil can either parry sixte, quarte—high septime, or even high quinte.

The Riposte

From the parry comes the riposte: an offensive action after successfully parrying the attack. It can be immediate or delayed, detached or with opposition. It is best to riposte when the opponent is still coming forward on his lunge, as then he has no time to recover. The manipulators are relaxed when projecting the point on to the target. Many commands, such as 'Parry quarte riposte' are given, but the pupil is not made aware of where he should be aiming. The fencer should be made aware of aiming the point at a given place, that is 'an opening line', and training should be given as such. If the riposte is delayed, make sure the opponent is not one who renews an attack, because by delaying the riposte, there is a period of fencing time lost; however, by delaying, the defender can see what line the attacker is going into, and while the attacker is closing one line he is opening another and that is where the riposte should go.

Fig 53   The lunge and parry quarte.

Fig 54   Parry riposte.

Fig 55   Parry quarte with point taken out of line.

Fig 56   Parry quarte riposte.

Fig 57 Foil. Winning hit in the final of Eden Cup. Angulated attack possible under an incorrect parry.

With a 'detached' parry (that is, after immediately parrying take the blade away to riposte) the riposte should be direct. From an opposition parry, the riposte depends on distance, and also on the opponent's reaction.

1. At a short distance, riposte should be direct.
2. At lunging distance, it should be direct or compound.
3. At a longer distance the riposte should always be indirect as a simple riposte would not succeed.

When training, it is best to start work at a short distance because it is important to learn to relax the arm when riposting. Imagine the point as a piece of elastic. It is extended in a smooth action by pressure of the thumb, therefore extending the fibre muscles, giving them a longer stretch. Test by jerking the arm out with fingers extended, which finish short of a wall. Next, stretch the arm out in a fluid motion and you will find the fingers touching the wall, because in jerking you contract (shorten) the muscle.

The coach should insist on a properly executed parry, so as to be able to execute a proper riposte by redirecting the point which finishes out of line. If the hand or arm moves, the riposte could land off target or miss altogether.

Fig 58 Extension of arm and aiming.

Fig 59 On parry quarte, the attacker has disengaged.

Fig 60 Parry quarte and disengage hit. No lean of body when hitting.

Fig 61 Parry on the lunge after the riposte.

To speed up the riposte, use your voice or speed up your parry, or even take a short cut by parrying early. The sound of the parry will also guide you to the success of the riposte. If the coach makes small movements, the pupil will also.

Counter Riposte

The counter riposte is an offensive action after successfully parrying the riposte or counter riposte. Odd numbers of counter ripostes are made by the attacker; even numbers of counter ripostes are made by the defender.

Fig 62 Counter riposte. Sword-arm hand above the level of the shoulder.

Fig 63   *Parry on lunge. First counter riposte.*

Fig 64   *First counter riposte. The lunge and parry.*

Fig 65   *First counter riposte. The hit after the parry.*

Fig 66   *A disengage lunge on parry of quarte.*

Fig 67   *A feint of straight thrust when opponent's blade is low.*

It is considered that the ability to make counter ripostes in a fight shows expertise because it shows skill in all its forms, controlled technique, co-ordination, timing and also tactical awareness to outwit your opponent. The more you practise counter ripostes, the more confident you become in your attacks and parries because you know that if the attack fails, you can fall back on the counter riposte.

To use it as a premeditated movement, lunge as though you are making the attack, but lunge short, draw the parry riposte, parry the riposte and drive home with the counter riposte.

COMPOUND ATTACKS

Compound attacks consist of two or more blade movements, each previous movement being a feint.

Example, from engagement:

- disengage, disengage (one-two)
- cut-over, cut-over
- cut-over, disengage
- disengage, cut-over
- counter disengage, disengage.

These can be done from all positions. With absence of blades:

- feint of straight thrust, disengage
- feint high and low
- feint low, come high
- feint of straight thrust or counter parry
- disengage (double) done on a counter parry.

A compound attack should be set up, and then executed without a pause. A compound attack requires complete dexterity of the manipulators and the ability to sell the movement you are making. For instance, if you wanted to do a 'one-two', make one or two false attacks to ascertain your opponent's parry. After deciding he does a parry of quarte from sixte, make a deep penetrating lunge as your opponent parries, relax the manipulators, dip your blade under your opponent's and hit.

This is where the progressive compound attack is important. At lunging distance and

Fig 68   Feint of straight thrust.

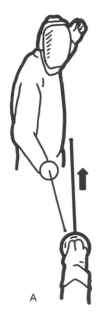 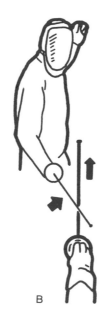 

Fig 69   The attacker attacks as in A, the defender parries as in B, no riposte so attacker disengages under and hits as in C.

sitting well down on your back leg to gather power, start with the blade movement followed closely by the front foot driving off from the rear leg. Draw the parry, deceive and hit at the same time as landing with the front foot. You should be in full acceleration when hitting your opponent. If you are too close, you will not have reached full speed, and if you are too far away, acceleration will have died down. Many compound attacks fail because of incorrect distance and lack of power in the lunge. People who lunge correctly are John Feathers, National Coach in Australia, Kirsten Palm of Sweden and Monicka Pulch of West Germany. If you can force your opponent to parry early, the more time and perception you have of his reaction parry, the better the chance of hitting him with a compound attack. Remember, the arm must be straightening and in line with the target.

Practise in pairs, first making one or two false attacks, the defender choosing any form of defence with his blade. The attacker then tries to deceive the defending blade. Next stage, do it progressively (with the blade travelling forward in one movement). Next, do it with an attack en marche. A big problem is that the attacker then fails to make his first movement penetrating enough and makes his second movement too early (before the other person has parried). In effect, the attacker has parried himself.

In training, you have two choices:

1. You lunge and hit.
2. You lunge as defender parries, you deceive and hit.

The defender must make the parry only when the attacker makes a deep feint.

Common faults include the use of the arm

from the shoulder. Large movements will slow down the attack, giving the defender a greater chance to do a successive parry. It will also increase the chance of your going off target. Make sure that you do not bend your arm while deceiving the opposing blade, except when doing broken time.

Broken Time

Broken time literally means time that is broken up by a pause in the normal pattern and it is intended to confuse the opponent. During the confusion, the attacker can place his point where he wishes. Broken time can be badly executed direct attacks such as bending the arm as you lunge, or a cut-over as an attack or a riposte. There could be a pause as the arm is brought back to disengage over the blade. To help eliminate this, do it only on a person on a low guard. Make more use of the manipulators and, also, if you engaged the person's blade first on the release, it will spring back giving you time to execute the movement.

RENEWALS OF AN ATTACK

In a fight between beginners, it will be noticed that one attacks and the other parries without riposting. The attacker renews the attack but because of poor technique, the defender is able to parry again. If the defender is in the habit of riposting, it is no good continuing with the attack. An experienced fencer can often be frustrated that an attack is blocked by a 'panic parry' because when danger threatens, fear can overcome many difficulties. Make sure that only the blade is deflected; do not follow the parry downwards. Relax the fingers, bring the blade round and replace the point. This is called the

redouble, that is renewing the attack in the opposite line or the same line. (Lines are explained in the section on simple attacks (see page 23).) Redoubles can be made with the cut-over, counter disengagement or disengagement. In the same line, the attacker can bend his arm and replace the point direct or by compound (for instance, one-two). The fencer can bring his rear foot up and angulate round the blade. Redoubles are often made at close-quarter fencing and one jabs away. As long as you can wield the sword the president will not call halt. A redouble can be classified as a premeditated attack: the attacker has seen the defender, does not riposte, attacks and does an immediate redouble after the parry.

Distance is another important factor: if you wish to disengage and are too close, you will not be able to keep your arm straight.

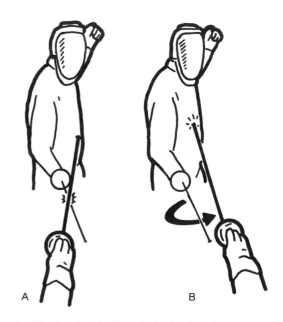

Fig 70   A redouble. The attacker beats as in A and lunges. When the defender parries as in B and does not riposte, the attacker disengages and hits.

Fig 71   Parry quarte, having stepped back just out of range.

The Remise

The remise is a renewing of the attack by replacing the point in the same line without any further action of the body or blade. When parried, relax the fingers when the defender takes away his blade; after the parry close the fingers and replace the point by pushing forward after the hit. Distance is important.

The Reprise

The reprise is executed either forward or backward by going through the on guard position and lunging again. This was the favourite movement of German fencer, Monicka Pulch, an aggressive attack that made her opponent retreat, followed by a fast reprise, or even two or three if the defender was in full flight. 'As in warfare, if the enemy is in retreat, keep at them; do not let them settle down and dig in.' Monicka Pulch won an Olympic Individual Silver and Team Gold.

With a reprise backward, knowing your opponent comes forward on your return to guard, replace the front heel and then lunge again. Execution of the reprise forward needs great flexibility of the rear knee joint; bend the rear knee, bringing up the rear foot, then lunge again. The main fault is use of the rear hip which brings the body up before lunging again. To prevent the body rising, practise the training exercise in Chapter 2 (*see* page 17), which involves suspending a beam over the head. Reprise forward.

Distance is an important factor. An exper-

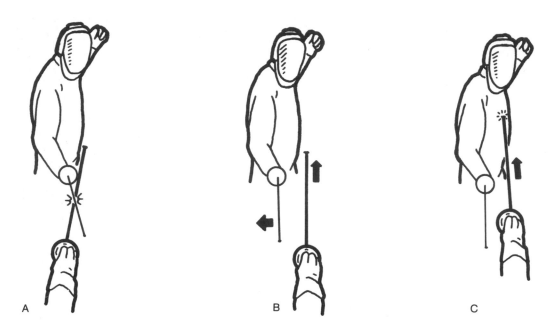

Fig 72   The attacker as in A parries when the defender takes away his
blade as in B. The attacker then replaces his sword i.e., the remise as in C.

Fig 73   The attacker has lunged, finds his opponent has stepped back,
brings up his rear foot and lunges again.

Fig 74   Finish of reprise forward.

ienced fencer will step back just out of reach, so the fencer needs only to bring the rear foot up a small distance. Somebody else might step further back so the rear leg needs to come up further. It is also possible to do a cross-legged reprise. When working together, step back only when the lunge is coming at you. If you step back before the lunge, the other person instead of doing a lunge followed by a reprise will do a step forward followed by a lunge.

PREPARATIONS OF ATTACK

Gaining and breaking ground; attacks on the blade; pressure, beat, graze coulé, prise de fer, bind, croisé, envelopment, froissement, reaction and deflection.

All movements that precede an attack are called preparations. They can be done with body or blade movements or a combination of both. The hardest thing to achieve when combining body and blade is co-ordination. You need to work body and blade together, and co-ordinate it cohesively. Movements of the body can also be complex so to begin with, it is best to keep movements simple. Preparations can also be used for defensive movements, such as a parry riposte or a counter riposte.

Many presidents cannot distinguish between an attack and a preparation. Some forms of preparation take priority, for ins-

Fig 75   An attack as an opponent lifts his front foot.

tance, the feint is immediately followed by the final movement. Other forms of preparation must be followed by the attack, such as a beat lunge. It is the most vulnerable time for the 'preparer' because his opponent can attack. Preparations must be practised a great deal, that is attack en marche, step forward, lunge or an attack could be executed on the step forward. The step must be small, followed immediately by the lunge. A step forward with a bent arm does not give priority, but if the opponent does not attack on the preparation, the right of way is still neutral.

Gaining and breaking ground can be done by the step forward, step back, balestra, jump-back, a cross-step or moving the rear foot closer to the front foot or a lean forward of the body. In doing backward movements, step back, taking the front foot further back nearer to the back foot in order for the body

balance to lean forward (as a preparation for a flèche).

The appel combined with a jump forward can cause a defensive action on the part of the opponent. The leg and arm movements can be done separately (double preparation) or together (compound preparation).

The Engagement

If your opponent has a sufficient angle to his blade, you will find it easier to engage in one of three places:

1.   With the foible to the forte.
2.   With the foible to the middle.
3.   With the forte to the opponent's foible.

By having the foible against the forte, it makes sure the opponent is properly covered, but leaves the attacker open to an

Fig 76   Engagement of blades.

attack. With both blades in the middle there is no advantage with the forte on the opponent's foible as one can open the opponent's line while being covered. Therefore, the engagement can prepare an attack by fixing the opponent's hand, followed by a pressure, a beat, or froissement, without a large movement of the hand.

The engagement can be used in attack to cause a reaction, taken well forward, started

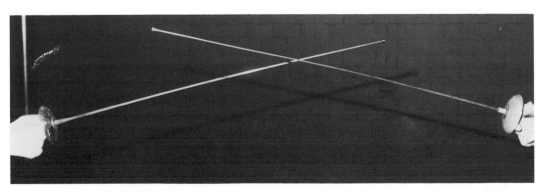

Fig 77   Engaged middle to middle.

strongly and followed through. It can provoke a counter-attack by making a larger hand and arm movement slower. Lastly, it can be done to provoke an attack. When engaging, start with the point, otherwise the hand could be deceived (dérobement).

Double Engagement

The double engagement involves two changes of engagement. One could be reaction followed by a deflection, or vice versa. The movement is done by manipulation of the fingers, the hand remaining still. Although I have mentioned engagements, they are very suitable for beginners and intermediates, as they control the on guard position. Some fencers like to do a change of engagement either to prepare the attack or to draw a response from the opponent, such as a counter disengage.

When fencers are more experienced, much work is done with absence of blade, and more use is made of feint attacks, false attacks, or attacks on the blade.

False Attacks

A false attack or second intention is a movement made to draw a response from the opponent to enable you to deliver the real intended movement. For instance, a half-

Fig 78   Foil. *Good position of lunge on right has caught the fencer on the left off balance.*

lunge can be used in order to draw a parry riposte while the real intention is to make a counter riposte by parrying that riposte, then hitting. You can provoke a counter-attack by doing an exaggerated preparation, then parrying and riposting.

In doing preparations it is important to maintain distance, also to have a good sense of timing and also to be able to co-ordinate the whole with the hand and leg movements.

Prise de Fer (Taking of the Blade)

Bind A diagonal movement high to opposite low and vice versa. When using the bind, the danger is of dragging the opponent's blade across and hitting off target. It is effective when used on a left-handed opponent who tries to dérobe your parry quarte: counter quarte bind to octave.

Envelopment A circular movement bringing the blade back to the initial line. The envelopment is mainly used at épée.

Croisé Taking of the blade vertically from the high line to low and vice versa.

Opposition A straight thrust down the blade without moving the line of the opponent's blade. Opposition is usually combined with a disengage, a coulé-disengage, as it keeps the opponent in line. At the last moment disengage with a relaxation of the fingers.

Prises de fer should not be done with a bent arm as it would be difficult to control the forte to the foible. They are best done as a riposte, counter-attack or remise. Prises de fer are useful as they control the opponent's blade during the action and you know where your opponent's blade is. You must realize the importance of controlling with the forte first by executing proper parries in the lines, that is in quarte your opponent's blade should be

resting on the top of your guard with the forte against the foible. If you pronate your wrist, you will allow the other blade to slip off; if you leave the blade behind leaving your fingers in supination, the blade will come through the gap left.

Try doing envelopment of sixte (a complete circle). The coach puts his finger to the pupil's point and makes sure it returns to the same place before riposting. In all these prises de fer check the start of the action, then the finish of the action before the hit. Practising the prise de fer, from sixte to quarte, bind to octave, envelopment of octave, then back by bind to quarte, envelopment in quarte, finish off by croisé in septime.

You must also be careful not to make too large a lateral movement, because it could evolve into a pressure. Simple dérobements will encourage small movements of the hand. Even though we have used prises de fer as a preparation, I think it best to mention now the defence to such movements, and they are:

1. The parry.
2. Avoidance of blade contact by derobing.

There are three different ways to parry:

1. By opposition, which allows the opponent to take the blade, sixte straight thrust and on the final movement bend the arm into sixte, covering the line. I found this movement difficult to use against the Russians, who really knew how to take the blade, but with the majority of fencers it is very useful.
2. By ceding, which involves keeping contact with the blade, but at the last moment taking control of where the prise de fer was to finish, that is quarte to octave, but cede into quarte. Left-handers like to cede into prime.
3. By counter parry, for example, counter sixte on quarte opposition.

Fig 79   Taking of blade in sixte.

Fig 80   Parry quarte.

Fig 81   Parry quarte croisé; hand lowered vertically.

Fig 82   Riposte by croisé. Forward leg leans into movement.

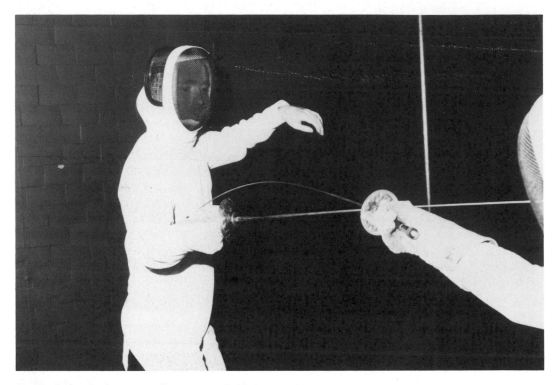

Fig 83   *Lunge in sixte, controlling opponent's blade.*

Attacks on the Blade

Beats

Beats take the form of either deflection or reaction. The beat done with the middle of the blade against the foible of the opponent should be short and crisp, like the sound of a clock ticking. If you turn your hand, you will get a sliding action and lose the effectiveness of the beat. The intensity of the beat should be strong to deflect yet light to react. In both methods it is the action of the manipulators with the aids controlling the sword. When beating with the middle of the blade, hitting with the corner will give a sharper beat than with the flat edge. Try the corner of the blade

against your finger, compared with the flat side, you will notice the difference.

Beats can be done in any line, but it must be noticed that the blade, not the movement of the arm, does the beat. If the arm moves, the opponent can deceive the blade and attack. With a partner, practise the beat—return—beat and listen to the sound of the beat. With practice, you should get the sound of a clock ticking. When you have the clock ticking away, one partner disengages as the other blade is on its way back. No movement of the hand is noticeable, just a relaxation of the manipulators.

A beat can be followed by a simple attack or a compound movement. Beats can be done from the disengagement; from a position of absence of blade; when the opponent

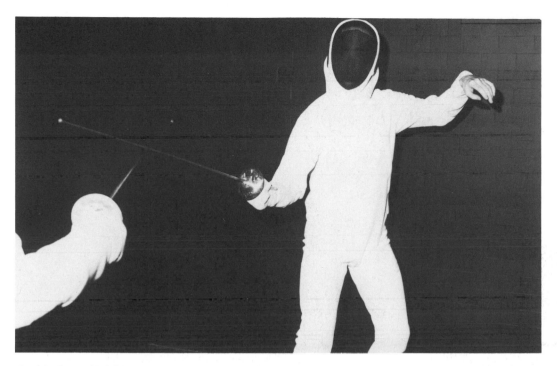

Fig 84 Beat with foible.

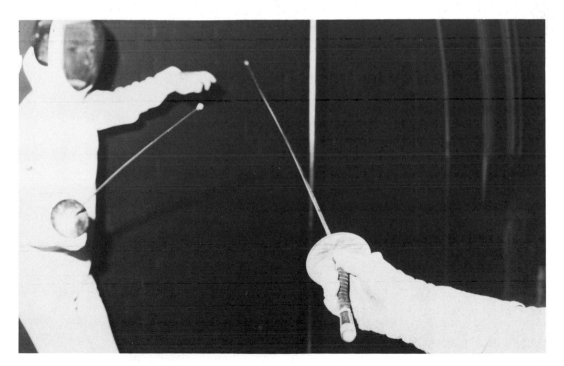

Fig 85 Relaxing of fingers after beat; no movement of hand.

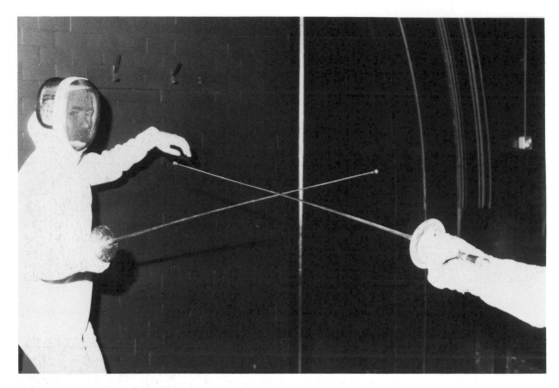

Fig 86   Beat in sixte.

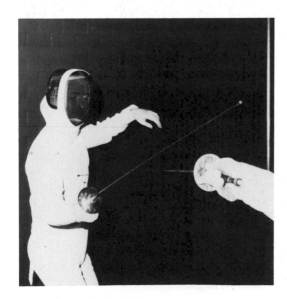

Fig 87   Extension in sixte.

moves his blade from one position to the other; and finally, from a change of engagement.

Double or Compound

These involve the co-ordination of hand and leg. The double is made with a beat to the blade while the compound preparation is made with a step with the front foot and a beat as the rear foot comes up. Movements should be short and sharp to gain time and distance. If, however, the fencer tries to provoke a movement, it is important that he maintain balance in order to react against an attack with counter-time or parry riposte.

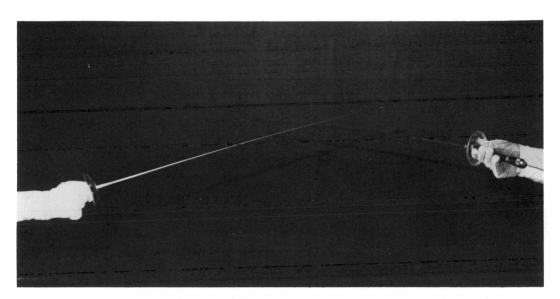

Fig 88   The beat in quarte.

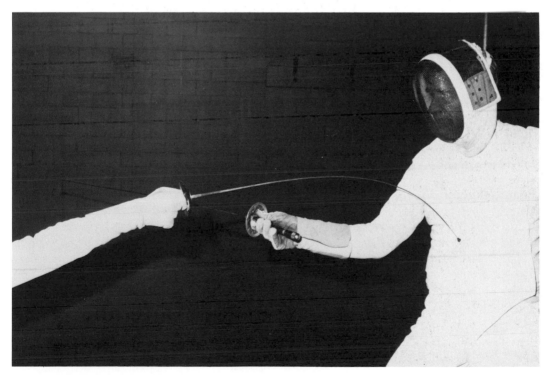

Fig 89   Beat deflection and lunge.

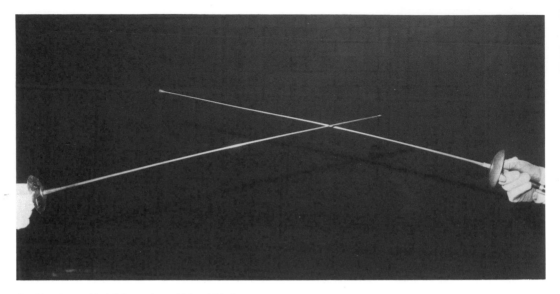

Fig 90   *Beat with foible on the middle of blade.*

Pressure

Similar to the beat, it is used to open or create a reaction. You can either intensify the pressure to follow with an attack or create a reaction to follow with a disengage. Exercises with the pressure are useful since they give you the feel of the blade (sentiment de fer) including the reaction of the opponent's parries.

Points to look out for Do not lean too hard on your opponent's blade — on release of the blade your blade could follow it. Also, do not put too much weight on the front leg. Another mistake that is noticeable amongst beginners is the raising of the elbow caused by the turning of the hand to pronation.

The Froissement

The froissement is a sharp action down the opponent's blade, displacing it by rotating the wrist into supination and doing a straight thrust. This movement is made against an opponent who has a weak guard, that is although the hand might be in position, the point points inwards.

Counter-Time

Quite often, an experienced fencer coming up against one of superior ability realizes that his attacks are failing, but has a chance with counter-time or second intention. Counter-time is an action to draw a counter-attack parry with a foot movement or a flèche. Counter-time can be done whilst in balance, in the on guard position, parry riposte, or out of balance while on the lunge. Fencers with a good hand or reflexes can do a reflexive counter-time.

Defensive Counter-Time

Fencer A does a preparation of attack; fencer B does a parry riposte; fencer A does a parry riposte.

Counter riposte with second intention:

Fencer A attacks short; fencer B responds with parry riposte; fencer A parries and ripostes, pushing home this time with the riposte.

Offensive Counter-Time

Fencer A makes a false attack; fencer B counter-attacks with a step back; fencer A follows up with a reprise.

Counter-time is a useful action because from the opponent's mistakes, it is difficult for the opponent to recover. Therefore, make counter-time actions simple with direct or indirect ripostes with or without blade contact.

Practise with your coach. After going through the mechanics of counter-time, step forward with a large engagement. The coach deceives the blade by dérobement, you then parry and riposte. Progress further with the coach stepping back so that you have to lunge; then use it as a choice reaction, making sure then that the point is travelling before the foot. Emphasis should be on co-ordination. Further progress can be made when the coach adds a parry and you have to do an indirect attack. Once you have got used to these movements, the coach can introduce an attack on the preparation, for instance, he can provoke an attack with an engagement of quarte with the front foot, then parry riposte. Now you have to concentrate on distance and co-ordination. As you become practised in this, the coach should counter-attack at different levels of the hand and line. As you become more expert, the coach should then give choice reaction, first without mobility, then with mobility, then to competition speed. If you make a mistake, go back to the beginning before working up

to a high speed. In time, you will succeed automatically.

In fencing, movements are not always what you expect them to be. For example, the counter-attack may be too slow, which makes it necessary to finish with a simple attack, or the opponent might answer the feint and finish with a compound attack. When these possibilities are added to choice reaction, followed by foot movements, you are making progress.

To make these movements succeed, you should be perfectly balanced. To do this, a coach can follow a counter-time action with a final parry riposte, with the pupil doing a counter riposte. Also, the coach could do a negative action, that is make no response to your provocation. The type of riposte can often be determined by the distance involved: parry—quarte—riposte at lunging distance: cut-over at a long distance and prime at a short distance.

COUNTER-ATTACKS

Often, beginners will counter-attack through blind panic because they cannot parry. If the attacker is unsuccessful, the beginner will often score. The expert fencer will use counter-attack on an attacker who:

1. Uses two-time action.
2. Makes badly executed attacks.
3. Attacks high.

The rules state that to be valid, the stop hit must precede the final of the attack by an interval of fencing time, in other words, the hit must arrive before the attacker has begun the final movement of the attack; it is never valid on a simple attack.

It is not a movement I teach beginners

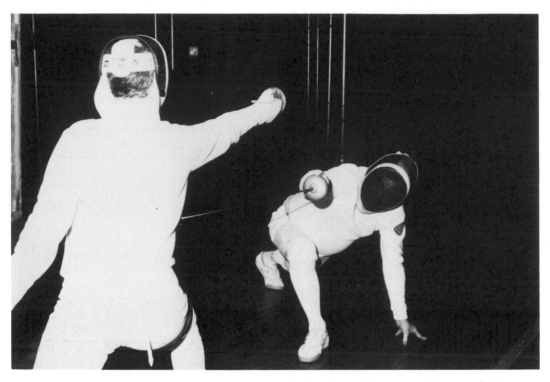

Fig 91   *Counter-attack by displacing the body downwards, but note that it is now illegal to place a hand on the floor.*

because it needs a deep understanding of timing and ability. Presidents also have many interpretations of a counter-attack. Many beginners will also extend their arm in a panic movement without parrying, so learning to parry riposte first is paramount.

If done properly, counter-attacks are of great psychological value against an opponent who likes to attack, but if used against an experienced fencer, beware of counter-time. To execute the counter-attack, you must anticipate what the opponent will do: broken-time movements, compound attacks or compound ripostes? At the early stages, you must learn when a counter-time is in time and when it is out. The counter-attack is more of a tactical movement.

The stop hit can be done with immobility, high line or a bending of the knees into the low line; side-stepping (inquatata) with a step back. Remember the difference between the attack into an attack and attack on a preparation (which are not counter-attacks). If the fencer has been taught to observe his opponent and actions as he withdraws his arm, he can counter-attack and then retreat. A fault of this is that the counter-attack is punched out and so the fencer is not relaxed to do a parry riposte in case of counter-time. Observation will also determine whether to do a counter-attack in high or low line depending on the position of the opponent's hand. A well-timed stop hit will stop an attacker dead in his tracks.

Fig 92   *Counter-attack by displacing
the body sideways.*

Compound Counter-Attacks

These are really for experienced fencers. Their purpose is to deceive a counter-time. It is difficult for an attacker to do more than one parry during the attack, because of the shortening of distance. Also it is difficult to do more than one feint, for example, a counter-attack by one-two. The attacker will not be drawn into parrying a counter-attack unless the counter-attacker extends his arm very early in a feint. To deceive the parry needs very skilful finger work. A very useful way of getting the attacker to react to the feint is by using the appel with the front foot. To assist

further with the success of the compound counter-attack, co-ordinate it with a step back, but it needs precise timing as the attacker has more room to resume his parries.

Stop Hit with Opposition and Stop Hit with Interception

There are two objectives:

1.   To hit the opponent.
2.   To deflect and control the opposing blade.

The stop hit with opposition closes the final line of where the attack is finishing. The manipulators place the point in the final line, followed by an extension of the arm. If you do it the other way round you could miss or find yourself counter-opposed. To reinforce the surprise effect, follow with a half-lunge, or with a step forward. Stop hits with opposition are not effective on bent arms or a cut-over. They are easier to execute in sixte and octave.

The stop hit with interception intercepts the attack before its final line of destination. Feint high, attack low. Counter-attack on the change of line, or as it crosses from one to another. To be effective, the counter-attack should start on the movement of the attack in order to meet the attacking blade at the right time and place. This can be used against an attacker who has been successful once, then immediately tries it again.

The difficulty of these movements means that if you parry too early, it can be deceived; if you parry too late, you are then parrying with the foible.

In practice, the coach can start with compound attacks, getting you to answer the feint to quarte, then intercepting into sixte. You must momentarily answer the feint into

Fig 93 Foil. The fencer on the right has attacked with a bent arm and front foot before the hand. The fencer on the left has a clear target to make a counter-attack.

quarte for the attacker to go into the second line.

Dérobement

I always say a fencer has committed hara-kiri if he launches an attack on a straight arm without deflecting it. If the person who has a straight arm bends his arm in the execution of the attack, he loses his right of way. The arm may move, but not bend. If the fencer evades the attempt by the attacker to seek his blade he has made a dérobement, but if he takes the point away from the valid target, he loses his right of way. To make this clear, the line must have been established before the attack is made.

Footwork has no relevant influence on the point in line, only the position of the arm and point. To save any argument, the less movement of the arm, the better; the dérobement should be done with the fingers.

To practise dérobement, start from the straight thrust. The coach should start with a slow lateral movement so that the pupil can operate the dérobement. He should make sure the pupil is successful by doing large movements, but he can vary the lines. To

Fig 94   Attacker on left has not lunged with power as rear leg is bent.
Fencer on right has left the piste, i.e. the right heel of the right foot is off
the ground.

increase the use of the fingers, practise two successive dérobements from an engagement and a beat. Check that the arm and shoulder are relaxed and that it is done with the fingers and no rotation of the hand. Do not lift the hand too high as the wrist will be too angulated, making the dérobement more difficult to execute against a beat. Do not thrust forward but let the opponent run on to the point; leaning forward with the body could make the point miss.

For a choice reaction exercise, if the coach does beat the line and extend, you must parry and riposte.

Fencers are often confused when they see a person with a point in line and even in the lunge position and they do not know what to do. The easiest thing is to do nothing, or even step back. You could stand still and make movements of the blade and you will see attempts to dérobe. By doing this your opponent's arm will get tired.

Another form of defence is to beat in order to provoke a dérobement, then change beat, which is difficult to evade. If there is difficulty in finding the opponent's blade, beat in high septime, as it is more difficult to dérobe because of the angles of the blades. During practice, ensure that the blade precedes the leg movements.

You should understand that when attacking and attempting to find the opponent's straight arm in order to deflect it does not succeed and the attack is continued and both hit at the same time, the person who dérobes is awarded the hit. Essentially the attacker has attempted to find the blade and has failed.

The dérobement needs good finger work, anticipation, timing, calmness and control. It is easier to dérobe from lateral preparations.

3 The Épée

Basically, épée originates from the duelling sword and so therefore, the whole body is the target. The scoring is also different to foil in that when both fencers hit at the same time, it is recorded as a double hit.

Épée was first introduced into the Olympic games of 1900, held in Paris. The year 1908 saw Team Épée introduced into the London Olympics. In 1936 the Electrical Scoring System was used first at the Berlin Olympics.

BASICS

The basics of épée differ from those of foil. Although in Britain fencers start on foil then transfer to épée, in Europe, it is épée first and last. The stance (on guard position) needs to be correct to protect against any direct attack to the advanced target, that is the arm. The stance also needs to be shorter than at foil.

The front knee is not so bent (so as to avoid attacks to the knee), and body-weight is on the balls of the feet, not on the heels as in foil. The body is upright, and the sword-arm further extended, but relaxed. The fore-arm is well covered by the guard and the hand is slightly in supination, that is thumb at one o'clock, point slightly below opponent's guard (octave position).

When practising épée, imagine you have a torch and keep the beam directed to the hand at all times. The result of this is that the guard protects the arm, the point, body and legs, and dérobements can also easily be performed.

Fig 95   The épée target.

Common faults in practising épée are as follows:

Body-weight too far forward.
Body-weight on back leg.
Stance too large.
Top half of body leaning forward.
Wrist bent as in foil, showing hand and forearm.
Sword-arm too extended, causing tightening of shoulder.

Fig 96   *Épée. A good attack to body, which has caught the fencer on the left in a poorly balanced position.*

The measure is different from that of foil:

1.   Long distance: advanced target (hand, wrist and forearm).
2.   Middle distance: knee or foot.
3.   Short distance: normal foil distance (the body).

Footwork

Duels in films show that footwork must be very mobile in order to hit on different parts of the body, and to avoid being hit.

Attacks

As at foil, the lunge and also the flèche are used at épée. With the flèche, an attack can be made from a long distance and, with a taking of the blade in high sixte to the body, leaves no room for a dérobement.

The Half-Lunge

The half-lunge is a useful method of provoking your opponent instead of a feint with a step. With this provocation, a compound

Fig 97   Hit to top of wrist.

Fig 98   Over hit to body; large bend in the blade.

Fig 99   Stop hit to under wrist.

Fig 100   Hit to under wrist.

movement can be executed. It is imperative in all attacks to have the arm behind the guard.

Return to guard either with the rear foot or front foot, is done with the arm extended and the point threatening the opponent's arm. If these movements are followed by a lunge, it is a reprise. In order to hit the various parts of the target, the épéeist should make use of simple or compound attacks, with or without preparations.

Firstly, straight thrust or disengage to the advanced target or with angulation. Secondly, simple attacks to the body by straight thrust or disengage. Looking at the technique — straight thrust at the wrist or forearm, on top, below, outside and inside, or disengage to the following places mentioned above. Make sure in all cases you are covered before lunging. If the opponent is well covered it is necessary to use a preparation.

Angulation Attacks

This is usually made at forearm or wrist and is a movement designed as a straight thrust with the final part angulated, getting the point over and moving the hand out of the way of

Fig 101   Épée. An angulated attack round opponent's parry.

the opponent, as the top of the hand is higher than the point. Underneath, the hand is lower than the point. For angulation outside arm, the hand finishes in pronation. For angulated hits on the inside, the hand finishes in supination.

Angulated attacks are recommended to fencers who have an extended arm. A sharp beat could help an angulated attack to succeed. For instance, beat quarte hit inside; beat tierce hit underneath.

Compound Attacks

These are attacks with two or more periods of fencing time. One with compound attacks. Next, attacks on withdrawal of the hand. As at foil, compound attacks deceive one or more parries. With the withdrawal of the hand, use offensive actions with one or more feints, finishing with a straight thrust as the opponent withdraws his hand.

When doing compound movements with one feint, you either finish at the most advanced target, the medium target or, finally, the body. If two feints are used, you would finish with the point at the body. Attacks made on the opponent's withdrawal of his hand finish either at the advanced target or at the body.

At épée, feints that are commonly used are simple, straight thrust or disengage; compound, one-two, double, top and below or below top. Feints are co-ordinated with opponent's engagement(s). Good leg action is necessary for the success of these attacks. All feints are combined with steps on half lunges and preparation must be careful, otherwise a counter offensive will score.

Finger play is important because any movement of the arm will uncover the target, therefore making it vulnerable to a counter attack and in compound attacks it is best to deceive the parries.

At épée, there is a greater appreciation of fencing measure compared to foil, owing to the advanced target.

In coaching the movement, the coach should find it easier to give the reality of actual combat.

Defence

The épéeist should adopt an offensive-defensive action concentrating on point thrusts. Except in long attacks where the foil parry can be used, it is chiefly parry riposte combine, that is opposition with the guard—riposte. Basically, the premier parries are ones that deflect the blade to the outside in sixte, counter sixte, octave and counter octave. The secondary parries are quarte, counter quarte, septime, prime and seconde. Prime is useful for prises de fer in sixte.

Whilst the short parry (used against long attacks) is identical to the foil, the long parry needs different techniques. There is more emphasis on the point action and it should also be executed with extension of the arm while at the same time retreating. Parries can be circular, semi-circular or direct. They can be done with opposition or ceding.

Against compound attacks use successive parries: sixte, counter-sixte, counter sixte-quarte.

Beat Parries

Depending on the position of the opponent's point, beat parries are made higher or lower than the hand. Without displacing the hand, beat sharply on the extended blade and riposte quickly to wrist or forearm. The riposte can be done with angulation so as to avoid the remise.

With short parries, as used in foil, parries must be executed with opposition. Limit the hand movement if you do move after the

Fig 102   *Épée. A good example of two fencers keeping the points in line.*

Fig 103   Parry octave riposte to body.

Fig 104   Parry octave deflecting blade and hitting the body.

Fig 105   Parry octave hit to knee.

*Fig 106   Good clearance by parry octave but the point is too low.
The arm should be further forward.*

Fig 108   Counter-attack. Hit to outside wrist.

distance. The parry is done with the arm extending and the prise de fer begun without stopping, but make sure the parry comes before the riposte and the prise de fer is not large. The counter-time can be parried and the attacker can then do a renewed attack.

Renewals

At épée, renewed attacks can be either offensive or counter-offensive.

The Remise

The remise is a replacing of the point in the same line of the parry. The redouble finishes in the opposite line or in the same line; there is no withdrawing of the arm. The remise is done on a straight thrust on the use of indirect riposte or after a compound attack, the use of successive parries.

The Redouble

This is done by disengage or two disengages. These movements can be done on a half-lunge, lunge with a reprise (forward or backward) with a flèche, returning to guard, or from the on guard position. With all lessons, the coach must make sure the pupil returns to on guard covered, correctly making him counter-attack, followed either by remise or redouble. This can be done by the coach threatening the target.

    Distance is an important factor. Counter-attack as coach advances, in continuation,

Fig 109   Ladies' épée. Fencer on left is holding pommel by the end; fencer on right has lunged within distance and also not covered herself when attacking.

so the pupil reprises. In getting the pupil to reprise only, the coach should step back during the lunge. If the coach goes too soon, the pupil will do a step lunge. Angulated hits in épée should only be taught when the pupil has sufficient expertise.

Attacks on the Blade (Preparations)

The Prise de Fer

Reference has already been made to prises de fer either in attack or defence but be-

cause of the advance target and the use of the counter-attack, the control of the blade is more important at épée. At épée, the use of prises de fer is done with a straightening arm because of the long distance; also, the blade should remain in a straight line with that of the forearm.

Points to look out for Arm and leg co-ordination. Use of too large a movement in trying to gather the prise de fer. Lack of opposition at the finish of the movement. When attacking, use prise de fer mostly in opposition and bind, finishing outside sixte and octave against a right-handed opponent.

Riposting   Riposting is used a great deal to avoid the danger of remise. For riposting, oppositions and croisé are used. It is dangerous to do a bind from septime to sixte or from quarte to octave since you are drawing his point across the body. Against a left-hander the opposite action is used.

The prise de fer should be done when the opponent's sword is extending, because if extended, there is a greater chance of a dérobement. To gain control, the forte must trap the foible or top of the guard. If not, there is a chance of losing the opponent's point. The movement must be completed before lunging or flèching.

At épée attacks on the blade are either:

1. To open the target.
2. To provoke a reaction.
3. To notice negative response.

Attacks can be made on the above preparations, either with the sword-arm extended for classical attacks or slightly bent for angulated attacks. Beats used are quarte and septime. Tierce and seconde, although strong, to uncover the forearm.

Pressures push the opponent's foil aside, followed by a simple attack, direct or indirect, but seldom compound, because of the counter attack.

The Froissement

This is a sharp displacement of the opponent's blade controlling it from foible to the forte. When against an opponent with a largely extended arm, only do the froissement from tierce and seconde. If you do not control the blade sufficiently, opposition can be applied to your blade, also a dérobement can be effected.

With attacks on the blade, you must develop finger play and arm and leg coordination. The coach can ensure that the beat is done on the last part of the footwork before the lunge to verify the balance of the pupil. Do a dérobement; if unbalanced, you will go on to the coach's point.

Be careful when doing attacks on the blade: ensure that actions are not too large with the hand or forearm and that you do not push too far after engaging the blade. Be sure that the attack follows immediately after the attack on the blade.

In practice, the pupil must find the target and this should not be made too easy. He must be made to learn to seize the slightest opportunity afforded him.

4 The Sabre

In Britain, foil is traditionally taught first. This is largely because most coaches are foilists and time and money do not encourage them to go further. But in Hungary, Italy and Russia, there are enough sabrre coaches for people to go along and start sabre. To Eastern Europeans there is the tradition of the light, mobile cavalry. Sabre in the army was a traditional cavalry weapon and was very heavy-handed. R.G. Anderson, the former Royal Marine competitor and National Coach, revived sabre fencing in England. Electric sabre, I think, will enable a phrase to be easily understood.

In recent years, sabre has fallen in popularity for several reasons. The main ones are lack of coaches, poor presiding and the numerous simultaneous attacks. The new rules ban crossing of the legs and fleching to cut down the number of running charges down the piste. Sabre should be taught separately because sabre movements are not the same as foil; the grip and also the manner of hitting are different. There are also different parries used.

One feature of sabre fencing is that compared to foil fencing, sabreurs seem more ready to practise movements. It could be because of the advanced target, and the fact that defence needs to be tightened (as is the case with épée).

Continued repetition of blade work, footwork and co-ordination of both, will result in precise execution of a stroke, giving time to think of a tactical approach.

The Grip

The grip is different from the foil. Cuts are made by presenting the blade to the target with the straightening of the arm, pulled back with the use of the little finger. Any swinging action will make the cut slow and also uncover your advanced target. Repetition cuts round the target should be practised.

The Target

Imagine riding on a horse. Everything above the level of the horse is the target; including head and arms. Below is 'off-target'.

The Stance

The stance is similar to the one used at foil except that the head is held more upright

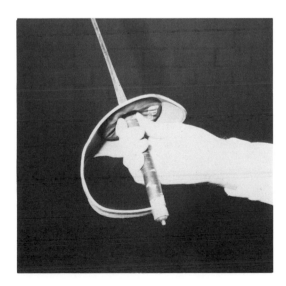

Fig 110   The grip.

Fig 111   The sabre target.

because of its being part of the target. The rear hand is placed on the hip to prevent its being hit.

Foot Movements

At sabre, short, sharp movements as of a sprinter are essential. Explosive exercises are needed in training for sabre. Attacks are made with rapid, short steps. The flèche and balestra are other commonly used movements.

As described in the foil section, the lunge is the driving force of the rear leg. The rear arm swings backwards and not sideways, otherwise the front shoulder will swing, causing the blade to miss.

Fig 112   On guard.

Fig 113   On guard defensive.

Fig 114   On guard offensive/defensive.

Distance

The measure is to that of your opponent's wrist. The flèche and balestra are that of foil.

Defensive Position

Forearm parallel to the floor; guard facing outward and point pointing further out.

Offensive-Defensive

This time with the blade diagonal across the body. This is also known as the Hungarian position.

Fig 115   Point hit.

The Hit

The hit is made in two parts:

1.   The arm is extended.
2.   The cut is made with the blade by pulling back the little finger.

Hits can also be made with the point.

Cuts

Cuts to the right cheek are made with the arm extended, at shoulder height, and the hand in pronation. Cuts to the head are made with the arm extended, the thumb on top. Make sure that the outside or underneath of the arm is not exposed by swinging or raising the hand. Cuts to the left cheek are made with the arm extended and the hand in half supination.

Cuts to the flank are made by extending the arm slightly down (not too far, otherwise opponent's cut will be made to upper arm). Point the blade down at 45° to the sword-arm, then use the fingers to cut. Do not bend the forearm as a stop hit to the arm will hit you.

Cuts to the chest are made by extending the arm in pronation and stroking down. This movement can be likened to a painter

Fig 116   The lunge.

Fig 117   Hit to head.

Fig 118   Cut to cheek.

Fig 119   Cut to flank.

Fig 120   Cut to chest.

Fig 121   Cut to outside arm.

Fig 122   Cut to raised arm.

Fig 123   Cut to inside arm.

stroking with a brush. Do not break at the wrist as it will pull the blade back. Return to guard immediately.

Hits to the arm should be angulated from the wrist so as to avoid being hit on the sword-arm, which is fully extended. With all these movements, repetitions should be made at various distances from short to very long distances. Always aim for precision before speed; if it breaks down, go back to a slower pace, then work up again. Start with one movement, then two, then a combination of movements. Feel the flow of the movement, the sound of the movements and the crispness of the hit.

Attacks

Attacks can be classified as in foil:

Simple or compound.
Tactical — real or false.
As a first intention or second intention.
Pre-planned.
'Open eyes'.

'Open eyes' means that the fencer has not pre-planned where he is going to hit and the final hit depends on his opponent's reactions.

Compound Attacks

A compound attack is made up of two or more blade movements. For example: flank—head, head—flank, head—chest. The position of the hand and arm is important because of stop-cuts. For a head feint, the hand is in semi-supination, level with the shoulder, the point is directed about 10cm (4in) above the mask. For a flank feint, the arm and the blade with cutting edge towards the flank; blade in horizontal position; the hand in pronation. For a chest feint, the arm and blade are extended with cutting edge towards chest; blade horizontal; hand in supination; palm uppermost. The point should be about 10cm (4in) above the target. If you do a head flank, feint to the head. As opponent forms his parry, rotate the wrist round and make the cut to the flank.

It is important to take movements simply so that you can progress to performing them with smoothness and efficiency. You must feel confident in the mechanics of the movement, combined with the footwork. These compound attacks can then progress to include a step; lunge—step, lunge; flèche—step, flèche—balestra, lunge—balestra, flèche.

These actions can be done standing still

Fig 126   Engagement in tierce and lunge.

attack on the preparation must start on the first movement to the head, either by lunge or flèche.

DEFENCE

There are two basic triangles: tierce, quarte and quinte; and prime, seconde and quinte (so quinte is common to both). With all parries, the blade is angled so that the opposing blade is gathered in to the hilt. When you parry quinte, the point is higher than the hand and so the blade will, when

Fig 127   Sabre. Fencer on right has hit to head with a lunge on fencer's preparation.

Fig 128   Guard of quinte.

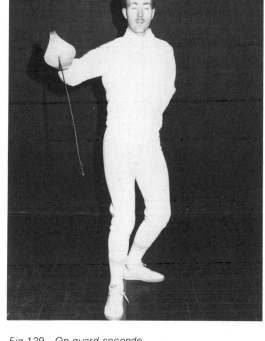

Fig 129   On guard seconde.

parried, slide in to the hilt and can be controlled when riposting.

For the low-line attacks, the sweep in to seconde or the parry of prime are being used more and more. In order to deceive, they have to disengage around the hilt. With seconde and prime, the arm is extended more than in tierce or quarte. In prime, imagine you are kissing the back of your hand. It should be the height of your shoulder, the blade angulated at 45°. With seconde the hand is lower, further out from the body, but the point pointing inwards and again at 45°. From seconde the two most used ripostes are to cheek and then to head. From prime, the most common ripostes are to the head, then to the chest. From quinte, riposte either to flank or head.

The following is a useful exercise: head

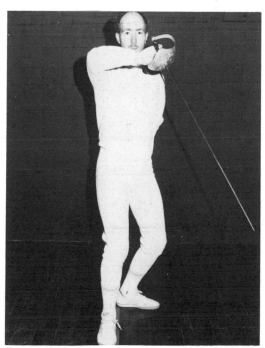

Fig 130   Position of prime.

Fig 131   Defence of quinte from cut to head.

Fig 132   Riposte to flank.

cut—parry quinte—riposte to flank—parry seconde—riposte to cheek.

Successive Parries

Tierce—quarte—tierce.
Tierce—counter—quarte.

Some movements can be done in two ways, either by using the hand and wrist in blocking the opponent with the guard, or by letting the point gather the opposing blade and taking it out of harm's way. Using the point is faster and can be used in a movement of second intention.

Ripostes

As at foil, ripostes can be direct, indirect or compound. Simple direct riposte is in the same line. Simple indirect riposte finishes in the opposite line to that of the parry owing to a simple deception either by disengage or coupé.

Here are a few examples of direct and indirect ripostes: From quarte *direct* to fore-arm—head—cheek—chest. *Indirect* flank. From tierce *direct* to arm—head—chest. *Indirect* flank.

Compound Riposte

This is any riposte or counter riposte preceded by one or more feints. For example:

Fig 133   Riposte to flank parried in tierce.

Fig 134　Riposte to arm after parry of quinte.

Fig 135　Sabre. Fencer on right has made a rare mistake: in parrying too
early he is deceived and hit on the arm.

parry quarte, riposte with feint to head, hit flank; or from tierce, feint to cheek, hit chest. After all ripostes, make sure the recovery is back to tierce, unless otherwise stated. Do call movements slowly at the beginning, then work up to high speed. You must be relaxed so that the movements flow. As at épée, the arm is the advanced target, so there must be no room for exposing the target.

Fig 136   Attempt to take the blade by counter of tierce.

Counter-Time Actions

Pupils step forward attempting to engage in tierce showing inside forearm. Defender stop cuts to inside arm. Attacker parries quarte, ripostes to head.

Counter Parries

Chiefly counter tierce, counter quarte and counter seconde. At sabre, the wrist and fingers describe a circle catching the opponent's blade, finishing with off the target. These circular parries are chiefly used against attacks to the arm, point attacks and beat attacks. As at foil, it is advisable to take a step back, as a circular movement takes longer than a lateral movement.

Fig 137   Cut to head. Stop point.

Counter-Attacks

Stop cut.
Stop cut with opposition and interception.
Dérobement.
Attack into the attack.

A stop cut with opposition is a counter-offensive action which closes the line into which the attack is directed. The most commonly used are those made on the chest with the point and on the head with a cut.

A compound attack finishing at flank: a

Fig 138   On preparation, stop cut to arm.

Fig 139   Dérobement with point hit.

Fig 140   Lunge to head. Attempt to stop cut to arm.

defensive action finishing in seconde with arm extension, scoring a hit with the point to the chest. The dérobement has been described in the foil section, but the hit can be made on the forearm.

An attack into an attack is only successful if the attacker misses. It is difficult because of the cut, but can be done with opposition, for instance, if the attacker does a step lunge to the cheek. The opponent also lunges, but blocks by opposition in tierce and scores a hit on the head. Ensure correct co-ordination between leg and arm movements.

Counter Offensive

Counter-Time and Second Intention

Most people think of these as being the same but counter-time applies to the way and situation of the action; second intention refers only to the tactical area of the situation before the action. So counter-time can be done as second intention or as a reflex action. With repetition actions, second intention actions could become reflex actions. They can be achieved either by parry or riposte. On a direct counter attack, parry with opposition on a simple or compound counter attack.

Counter-time can be done as an offensive action. For instance, while flèching, the attacker makes a parry while moving and ripostes. As a defensive action, the attacker stops to make a parry, then ripostes without any further movement.

There are three parts to a counter-time action: first, the preparation — probably an invitation to an offensive action; next, the defensive action; and finally, the riposte. The preparation is of importance because if it does not gain the response that is needed, the opponent will not respond. If the prep-

aration is overdone, the counter offensive action will score, especially with an advanced target.

In practising the counter-time, there should be a distinct change of rhythm. The preparation should be done rapidly, followed by a pause before parrying the counter attack; then the riposte should be made rapidly. With practice, the whole action will be smooth.

There are many examples of second intention. Step forward in tierce, opponent feints to inside arm, disengages under arm on the parry to outside arm on parry quarte, followed by parry to tierce and riposte by flèche to head.

With defensive second intention, the attacker makes a running attack; defender reacts with a parry; attacker finishes his attack into the opening target; defender is prepared, adds a second parry, then ripostes. This action cuts out trying to guess where the attack is going to finish.

In practising the variations of counter-time, it is best to practise a few and be good at them than practise too many and achieve only a low standard.

The Line

As at foil, the arm is straight with the point in line (threatening the target), hand pronated. In order to obtain right of way, the blade must be deflected, either by beat, engagement or parry. The blade in line can be followed by the dérobement, an action taken to evade the contact by the opponent. In order to keep the right of way, the arm must remain straight and the point still threatening the target. A good time to use this is on a running attack when the opponent is attempting to find the blade; at foil there needs to be exclusive use of the fingers.

Regularity

It is important to remember that regularity is not how often you do a programme, but for what period of time you perform it, i.e. programmes should start and end at the same time each session. The effect of the physical and psychological training is that it allows you to get proper rest and to prepare mentally for the next session. Programmes can vary, in the numbers a day or week, but keep them regular and consistent. This also helps in measuring progress.

Frequency

This depends on the work load needed and the intensity and response to the work load. The coach should be able to notice whether the frequency should be reduced. Frequency depends on how well the fencer responds to the exercises. Generally, low intensity training in any of the four muscle responses may be per formed several times a day without harm, but as the intensity changes and overloads, greater rest periods are needed. Specific goals and workout times may have to change or remain as they are, but it would be better to establish a new set of goals.

For fencers who have not had a sporting or athletic background, a frequent low-intensity programme should be adopted for a considerable length of time.

Adaptation

'I am not going anywhere; in fact I seem to be getting worse', is a common statement among sportsmen. When you do a physical programme, your body has to adjust and condition itself. Therefore, it is not uncommon during the early stages of training to go back in performance.

If you understand this and continue or revise your programme, you will overcome this hurdle and finally make progress. Psychologically, it can become a barrier; approaching the problem from another angle can be helpful.

Some people reach a plateau and then appear to get stuck. This is also another phenomenon of nature.

Progression

Step by step, progress towards a goal. It can be compared to climbing a mountain; it gets harder nearer the top but you can reach it. Do not rush to achieve your goals, but pursue them systematically and attain them degree by degree.

Overload

Stepping up the stress intensity of an exercise to achieve a higher level of muscle response is called overloading.

Increased intensity can be achieved by the four Rs of exercise. They are:

Resistance
Repetition
Rate
Rest

Resistance

The force or weight needed to overcome muscular contraction could be that of a body part or even of the entire body. Greater resistance comes from gravitational or leverage disadvantages, for instance, the resistance exercised before the lunge. Strength is measured by the amount of weight a muscle can overcome. Resistance exercises will help.

Repetition

Repetition is the number of times a skill is performed correctly. Increase in the number of repetitions will give you automatic response without having to resort to a thinking process, which leaves you time to concentrate on other problems.

Rate

Rate is the number of repetitions per unit of time. Rate is generally designed to increase stress tolerance and endurance and produces greater flexibility.

Rest

Rest is the time period allocated between different exercises. The harder the stress, the longer the rest. Some marathon runners only do three or four races a year.

Rest should also be a time of relaxation and you should learn to relax immediately. This improves the effectiveness of recovery from fatigue.

The type of rest found in interval training is of shorter periods as the body develops a greater resistance to fatigue.

Paarlauf training is working in pairs: one works full out and his partner relaxes with him. Then they change over, for instance, one fencer attacks, the other defends and then they change over.

Warm-Ups and Warm-Downs

Warm-ups are designed to improve the circulation, progressively stretch the muscles, improve freedom of motion and finally prepare the body for more vigorous action.

When a nerve or a muscle is cold it is more likely to snap, which could cause serious damage. I have seen a shuttlecock hit a person on the head when very cold and cause a stroke. Additional benefits to warming up are the promotion of relaxation and increase of self-awareness in readiness for the future activity.

Warm-downs are a series of short exercises to relax the muscles and promote some immediate removal of fatigue. They aid in reducing muscle soreness that may follow a work out.

Flexibility

Flexibility aids a range of motion and muscle responses. Flexibility should not be used as part of a warm-up programme. Movements then become awkward and jerky in varying degrees and as a result, the fencer is likely to have difficulty in being consistently fluid in his actions. Lack of flexibility often produces over-tense muscles. Tight muscles also cause pressure on the blood vessels and prohibit the blood flow. This prevents oxygen from reaching all the cells, thus limiting the performance especially in endurance tasks, like a complete day of fencing.

If your arm gets tired holding the sword, pump your arm a few times (bend it backwards and forwards). This helps pump oxygen into the muscle. Flexibility exercises are important, especially after an injury or sprain, or even after a major operation. Flexibility produces:

1. Strength, speed and endurance through the whole range of motion and greater gains in all three.
2. Improved ability to practise and also learn a skill.
3. Greater efficiency in performing a skill. Improvements in co-ordination, agility, quickness (including quickness of the mind).

With flexibility, a muscle can move through its entire length easily and efficiently. When all muscles round a joint are flexible, the joint can move through its complete range of movement.

Exercises

There are three types of exercise: rhythmic, static and exercises to encourage pain resistance.

Rhythmic

Rhythmic exercise includes flexibility exercises in their simplest form: arm circles and leg swings and serve as a mild warm-up. Do rhythmic exercises just to keep trim in the off-season so as to keep fluidity of movement.

Static

Static exercise means staying in a set position for a given time. Static exercises can be done in pairs and can also be done without a lot of equipment. You can work to your own ability. Simply select an exercise, for example, arm extension. Learn how to perform the extension properly, then using the principles of exercise, set out to achieve your goals in speed, endurance, strength and flexibility. The following points should be remembered:

1. Perform correctly, but do not try to make progress too rapidly.
2. When stretching your limb muscles, make sure you stretch the opposing ones.
3. If one set of muscles is particularly tight, stretch the opposing ones first.
4. Use a complete stretching programme. Do not confine it to one area because one muscle group is related to another. For example, back muscles are related to the leg and shoulder muscles.

5. Always precede flexibility exercises with simple calisthenics so as to stimulate circulation. Skipping is useful because it also brings in co-ordination and speed with endurance. Heart rate should be brought up to 100 beats per minute before starting flexibility exercises. Lastly, keep warm. Warmth enhances the benefit of exercises.

Pain Resistance

Stretch pain will cause tension and discomfort. Recognize it as a feedback from your body and use it to your advantage. In your mind have a pain tolerance of 1—10. When you first use a stretch programme allow yourself a low tolerance. Over several days, gradually increase the intensity of your effort and pain tolerance.

At all times, pay attention to the kind of stretch pain you experience. By paying attention to this, pain will identify the needs of the muscles. You will be able to recognize the difference between tension, pains that are relaxed, pains that need rest and pains that can be exercised. As you get to understand muscle pain, your ability to make progress in exercise you were afraid of doing improves; you will be able to relax away pains that stopped you from proper exercise, and exercise pains that you once thought were injuries. If you are able to recognize symptoms, you can prevent injuries before they happen and also gain greater confidence in performing a movement skill.

Relaxation

Learn to relax while stretching. Breathe normally; do not hold your breath; relax your way through an exercise and go on with the exercise. Concentrate and develop your ability to perform a specific task. Hold for short periods of time, but never longer than ten seconds and increase the number of repetitions of the exercise. Perform the exercises standing, seated and lying down. Keep the exercise programme flowing.

Concentration

When doing exercises, do not let outside factors interfere with what you are doing. Try concentration exercises or body control exercises. While the pupil stands on guard, the coach can help him to develop concentration by deliberately trying to distract him; the pupil must focus on the task in hand.

Do Not Bounce

A professional coach when told it is not good to bounce said: 'I've always done it and it is good enough for me'. Because he thought it was good enough for him, he had the answer. Why shouldn't you bounce? It does not allow the muscle to sustain the stretched length and benefit from it. It activates the stretch flex, thus causing the muscle to contract, rather than adapt to the stretched length. This promotes the opposite desired effect of shortening the muscle instead of lengthening it. Bouncing is dangerous. It can cause injury.

Resistive Flexibility

Resistive exercises not only improve flexibility, but also strength. Choose a partner of similar size, build and strength to yourself. Perform the exercises properly and to the best of your ability. Use a complete stretching programme and keep warm while stretching. Keep your clothing on and work in a warm area. Always stimulate circulation first. Perform exercises smoothly; do not jerk or snap the movement. Start with short ranges of motion building up to longer ranges

of motion. Do not start at the tight area, work up to it. Start with low pain range, stretch, then increase. Start with low resistance, work up to a higher level. Concentrate on your work. Pay attention and plan your progress.

BASIC MOVEMENT COMBINATIONS

Fencing, like boxing, deals with a combination of foot and body movements. Not enough emphasis is put on the pattern of movements.

Running long strides
Running short strides
Backward running
Side stepping

Pattern running Combine forward, backward, side step in lined drills over prescribed patterns, which include reverses, veers, directional changes and circles. Use lines, cones and bodies as markers.

Jumping Skills

Hops Single leg, double, alternate.
Jumps for distance Single leg, double, for standing single leg, double, vertical. Running long jump. Concentrate on balance. Tuck jump. Pike jump. Straddled toe jump. Jump with twist. Set out pattern of jumps in sixty seconds. Repetitions.
Skipping Rope Single leg. Double leg. Running while skipping. Count the number of skips in one minute.

Balance Skills

1. Single leg balance. Foot to knee, hold for ten seconds. Leg to side, front and rear, keep body as upright as possible.

Fig 155   With support, lift leg and hold.

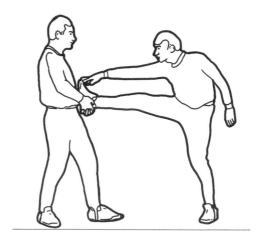

Fig 156   With a partner supporting the leg, touch toes with right and left hands alternately.

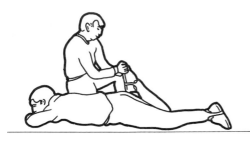

Fig 157   Partner kneeling alongside, bending foot back as far as possible.

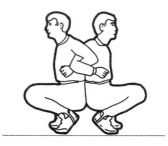

Fig 158   For this exercise, both people should be of the same size and build. Straighten and bend, trying to get a rhythm going.

Fig 159   Bending down touching the floor, stretch and bend the leg several times. Repeat with the other leg.

Fig 160   Lunge position; body upright. Stretch up and behind and hold. Repeat with other arm.

Fig 161 *Hands clasped, bend back and hold for ten seconds.*

Fig 162 *Hands clasped, push fingers away, then turn hands over.*

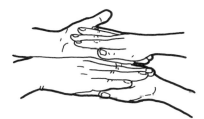

Fig 163 *Static resistance. Arms outstretched, one palm up, one palm down. Press and hold. Keep it static for one minute and then change palms over.*

Fig 164 *Partners should be of the same size and build. To make it harder, the person on the back can walk up with his feet so that his head touches the floor between the other person's feet. Take it easy!*

Fig 165 *One foot forward, hands against the wall, bend arms and hold, then straighten.*

2.   Hand and leg balance (frog balance).
3.   Moving balances (handstand).
4.   Single and double-leg hops over lines or obstacles.

Reflex Orders

From running around, on command get to 'get set' (on guard) position.

DRILLS FOR QUICKNESS AND AGILITY

Tuck jump on landing; spring 5 yards. Straddle jump on landing; run backwards 5 yards. Jump with full twist, sprint 5 yards and then jump again with full twist on landing; go into lunge position. Full twist right, sprint 5 yards, full twist left, sprint 5 yards; assume on guard position. Full twist right, tuck jump, full twist left, pike jump, sprint 5 yards.

Agility Drills

Twisting run followed by forward sprint.
Backward run followed by forward run.
One-leg hop, followed by sprint, followed by two-leg hop.
Back crab circle once left, once right, front crab once.
Front crab once followed by sprint.

Post Drill

You will need four cones placed in a square:

Run to cone 1, place right hand on cone and circle right.
Run to cone 2, place left hand on cone and circle left.
Run to cone 3, place right hand on cone and circle right.

Run to cone 4, place left hand on cone and circle left, then sprint to finishing line.

This drill improves balance, speed, acceleration and also quick change of direction.

Muscle development exercises combined with concentration on basic movements will develop total fitness in a fencer. The fencer will learn about human movement and also avoid injury. The fencer will acquire suppleness, elasticity and maximum range of movement. Muscular control will improve and also co-ordination. Very importantly, he will be nimble and light on his feet.

The programme, kept fresh, exciting and competitive will improve your mental attitude, which in turn includes self-discipline, confidence, determination and poise.

CO-ORDINATION

A useful exercise to improve co-ordination of the feet is a Philippine dance. For this, you will need two swords, body-width apart and placed on the floor, and a partner. Your partner should tap them twice on the floor, then bring them together, keeping the blades parallel. In the meantime, you have to step in and out before they come together. Start by having the right foot in the air over the gap in the blades. On the word 'go', place the right foot down, then up. As you place the right foot down on the outside of the sword, lift the left foot up and down in between the blades, lifting it up before the blades come together. Repeat going back, face the person with the blade.

To improve co-ordination of the arms, have both arms to the side. Lift right hand to shoulder. Lift left hand to shoulder; at the same time, right hand goes straight up. Left hand goes up; at the same time, right hand comes back to shoulder then left hand. As left hand comes back to shoulder right hand goes out to front, then left hand comes back to shoulder, right hand comes back to shoulder, left hand goes out. As left hand comes back to shoulder, right hand goes out to side. As right hand comes back to shoulder, left hand goes out to side. Right hand goes down, left hand comes back to shoulder and then goes down to side.

Bad co-ordination in fencing results in poor performance. A study of physiology will show that each muscle and joint, if moved in co-ordination, will result in a smooth, relaxed action giving full speed, strength and balance.

Fencing needs the added skill of the separation of the arm and leg movements. It might seem very laborious doing various exercises with the foot and arm, but these should not be done in a robotic manner. It is important to understand the reasons behind the movements, such as extending the arm at different times in order to become aware of timing with the action in relation to the legs. For example, practise extending the arm:

Before a step.
On the movement of the first part of the step.
On the second part of the step with the rear leg.
At the beginning of the lunge.
At the end of the lunge.

With all movements of co-ordination, you should try and get into bout situations, so it is important to link these together to make smooth movements. Too great a separation will inhibit the final result.

6 Well-Being

Medical diagnosis and treatment is best left in the hands of experts, as a little knowledge can be dangerous but there are things that can be done while waiting for help to come: first ask if there is anyone present with medical knowledge. Fencing is a sport that has very few injuries and full training reduces the risk still further. There are various factors that influence the chances of sustaining injury.

Age

With increasing age, there is a loss of elasticity of tissue and brittleness of bone. Bruises take longer to disappear; cuts take longer to heal. To stave off the ageing process, conscientious training must be kept up.

Temperament

The average fencer does not like training. Fencers often say that they fence for pleasure and do not mind if they lose, but watch them when they win. It is natural to feel good when aims are achieved. The coach should motivate pupils to greater achievements. Some essential requirements are alertness and quickness of thought, analysis of your opponent, and a tactical brain.

From this comes a variation in approach to a problem and a particular style. Many fencers are very enthusiastic at the beginning and wish to do more than they are capable of. This enthusiasm must be controlled to attain steady improvement.

Life-Style

Smoking

There is a lot of argument for enjoying a smoke; world champions and famous athletes have smoked, but there is increasing scientific evidence to show that smoking reduces physical condition. It is obviously best never to start but determination to stop could also help to develop determination in your fencing.

Alcohol

Alcohol is a depressant and not a stimulant. Everything in moderation is fine and socially enjoyable, but the self-discipline of being teetotal is all to the good.

Sleep

For each individual the required amount of sleep differs. In a sound sleep, the mind relaxes and is clear on awakening. There is muscle relaxation and you should feel raring to go. Lack of sleep leads to lack of muscle response and overall physical and mental fatigue.

Over a period of time, you can adapt sleeping habits. For example, a shift worker will be able to sleep during the day. Fencers between rounds can relax and nod off.

A fencer might not realize, especially at the Olympic games, that if he is used to living in the country where it is peaceful, staying in an Olympic village can be disturbing.

The type of bed in which you sleep is also a factor influencing quality of sleep. At a hotel, the bed might be different, so your skeleton rests differently and certain muscles remain tense, thus the feeling that the bed is uncomfortable, which results in certain limbs being stiff and aching. The criteria for rewarding sleep is not necessarily the amount, but the quality.

Drugs

It has been proved that drugs are harmful. Some might artificially improve performance for a time, but later on in life there are many side effects. The most common drugs are those found in tea and coffee. Little is known about the extent to which too much tea or coffee shorten one's reaction time since there is always a time lag between intention and actual doing.

Diet

Fencing requires a considerable amount of energy. We get energy from the quantity and quality of the food we eat and drink. The higher the quality of food, the better energy we can expel. With young fencers, it is a matter of building the framework of bone and muscle. Sometimes a teenager who has been doing well suddenly has an off period; this is often caused by energy being diverted into the growing process. When choosing a diet, it is important to have sufficient amounts of the following:

Calories
Carbohydrates
Proteins
Fats
Salts
Vitamins
Fluids

Since proteins are not stored in the body, extra protein is wasted, so, for example, steaks are not essential for fencers, but are useful for weight-lifters or boxers for building bulk. When fencing over a prolonged period, one day or two, it is imperative to have an energy reserve prepared.

Fluids are absorbed during activity, so remember to drink plenty and thus prevent dehydration.

If the diet has been properly prepared and the athlete has trained, sticking to that diet, the taking of extra glucose is of no benefit because the body already has ample supplies. Psychologically, a person can enhance his performance by thinking that a 'carrot will make him see better'. But remember that during violent exercise, the stomach does not want to be churning around a lot of food. With adequate regulation of diet, there is a full store of energy when required. In a trained person, it is not used as fast as that of an untrained person.

Nutrition during Competition

Most fencers take food along to competitions or have refreshments there, but they do not give sufficient thought to the sort of diet they should be having the rest of the time. Not all that is liked is compatible with competition. Sensible foods to take along to the competition are: wholemeal bread, butter, peanut butter, dried fruit, raw vegetables, nuts, cheese, bananas.

Fencing leads to a loss of water and certain minerals and carbohydrates are used up: these must be replaced. Perspiration occurs, particularly with the amount of equipment a fencer wears but instead of releasing his clothing, the fencer should cover up. When taking water, small doses are better than large ones.

The body needs protein, to be found in foods such as eggs, milk and fish. It needs vitamins, minerals and iron. Since the brain needs glucose as a fuel, sugar is required; honey is a good nutrient during a competition. These carbohydrates are stored and used during the competition.

Pre-Competition

Three weeks before a competition, load up with carbohydrates. For example, two meals of the day might typically consist of:

Fruit juice; cereal, milk and sugar; toast and coffee.

Small steak; baked potatoes, corn, salads; chocolate pudding; coffee.

Too little is much better than too much. A large meal before and during rounds can hinder performance. Eat easily digested foods and avoid gassy foods.

Four hours before competition:

baked potato, lean meat, peas, pudding, biscuits and milk.

One hour before competition: chocolate bar, fruit juice.

As most competitions start early in the morning but involve a lot of travelling, it is important to have a good breakfast of fruit juice, cereals with milk, egg, bacon, fried potato, tomato and mushroom, followed by honey on toast and coffee.

Glycogen

Fencing involves bursts of activity and therefore, glycogen is important to fencers. When glycogen breaks down, lactic acid forms as muscles are without oxygen. Shake (pump) muscles in order to restore oxygen. Lactic acid soon becomes evident in a non-fit person. Training helps to keep a lower lactic level, increases work capacity and also reduces recovery time. A trained fencer can maintain lower blood pressure and lactic acid levels during moderate exercise.

Therefore, correct diet and training can enhance the well-being of a fencer and thus improve his performance.

FIRST AID

St. John's Ambulance will provide cover in any fencing competition, but at club evenings, it is advisable to:

1. Know where the nearest telephone is.
2. Have a first aid box with a list of contents.

Contents should include:

first-aid book
bandages of different widths
crêpe bandages
strapping plaster
triangular bandages
cotton wool
gauze
safety pins
iodine
eye bath
jelly for burns
collodion (this forms a skin over cuts and limits bleeding)

The coach should try and get to know if any of his pupils suffer from a medical condition, such as asthma or any other disability. Any disabilities should be kept in mind during training.

Injuries

Bruises

Bruises can be kept to a minimum by massaging the affected area. For bigger bruises, apply a cold water compress. If a rib is cracked or fractured, see a doctor immediately and avoid exercise.

Cramp

Cramp is a muscle spasm brought about by an extreme or sudden movement and is a common complaint amongst fencers. To help prevent cramp, warm-ups are important, especially at a cold time of the year. Muscles under exercise require an increase of blood supply to perform well. This blood supply carries oxygen which removes lactic acid caused by fatigue. If the blood supply is restricted to the muscles, lactic acid builds up as the blood vessels contract. A recent meal can bring on cramp as the stomach requires an increased blood supply, therefore, a decrease to the muscles. Likely trouble-stops for cramp are usually the thighs, or less mobile limbs compared to the upper body, or the extreme ends, fingers or toes. Those fencers that grip their foil too hard can finish up with cramp, so it is important to make sure you have the right grip. A tense muscle tires more rapidly than a relaxed one, so coaches should introduce relaxation into their training programmes. To treat cramp in the legs, massage from the direction of the heart. Get the person up and walking so that the blood flows to the muscle.

Unconsciousness

It is not advisable to smack the cheeks or give smelling salts to an unconscious person. Roll a blanket with one end under the person, roll the person over carefully with the blanket, then lift via the blanket on to a stretcher. On no account drag the person. If no stretcher is available and you have to move the person, get alongside, one under the legs, two under the body and one supporting the head and shoulders and lift like a log. If in doubt, leave alone, but put a coat or two over him to keep him warm.

Injuries to the Ankle

A faulty lunge or an unbalanced movement can cause a twisted ankle. The two ligaments most often involved are the deltoid medial ligament or the anterior and it is usually the weaker anterior ligament that suffers. Swelling follows, so water compresses should be administered with the foot kept above the level of the leg. Until you receive treatment, keep your shoe on as it keeps the swelling down and is a support to the foot. Severely torn ligaments take a long time to heal, perhaps over a year, but regular exercises and flexion aid muscular strength and go towards preventing injuries.

The Knee Joint

Many fencers retire because of knee injuries caused by the constant jarring of the lunge. Three bones form the knee joint: the tibia, the femur and the knee cap in front. The lining of the bone surfaces is protected by cartilage. This acts as a buffer when force is used. The knee has two other cartilages which lie on top of the tibia where it comes into contact with the femur, so these cartilages cushion any force when lunging. Lining the joint is a thin tissue called synovium. This provides the fluid which oils the joint and, if injured, expands to cushion the joint and prevent further injury. If at the beginning of the season a swelling occurs, it is because the synovium has been trapped owing to vigorous exercise without proper pre-training. The knee joints will be better able to tolerate incredible demands on them if the quadriceps are in good condition.

If you lunge with your body turned sideways and your foot turned inwards, you could cause damage to the lateral ligaments of the knee joint, causing a forced rotational action to the side of the knee. If the pain is severe, see a doctor, but keep the joint moving.

Injuries to the Cartilages

Not all injuries are related to cartilage trouble but in fencing, with its bent position and often incorrect lunging or movement, cartilages can easily get torn. If they do, see a doctor. He will either trim or remove them. To leave them torn can cause later problems that cannot be cured. Subconsciously, you will use the other leg more, which causes muscle wastage in the bad leg, resulting in loss of balance and also recurrence of the problem. The stability of the knees rests on the strength of the quadriceps so as to cushion any jarring.

Fencer's Elbow

Pain develops on the inner elbow where the flexor muscles of the wrist are attached. It is a condition that is built up over the years. Massage by an experienced person is advisable, as is prolonged rest.

Rehabilitation

A fencing coach is not expected to have extensive medical knowledge but it is good for the pupil to know that the coach cares and can offer some advice. Swimming is good for rehabilitation as it gives full active muscle contraction, also full active joint movement, important for recovery.

7 Club Organization

Many a complaint is that people do not know where to go and join a class but the Amateur Fencing Association Headquarters (*see* Useful Addresses) will be able to give you the name of the secretary of your section. Alternatively, a good source of information is the library service, which will have the names and addresses of several clubs, including their opening times. If you are a beginner, it is also advisable to look at the evening classes. These are not usually clubs, but classes run for beginners where tuition and equipment are provided. Shop around until you find a club that suits you. You might have to travel, but it could be well worth it.

If you wish to learn and enjoy learning, especially technical skills, join a class. One advantage of fencing is that you can practise at home, so do get yourself a foil.

As you get better, other fencers will join your club and you can help them. It is often valuable to see the sort of mistakes they make and it makes you aware of tactical movements that could be used against beginners.

Coaches and advanced fencers do not often make good committee people — they are too busy coaching, or improving their standards and competing.

In a club, leaders will emerge and it is advisable for them to run their own section. If that cog or section is not running well, one should be replaced immediately.

As far as advertising your club is concerned, seek professional advice. If you are lucky, one of your members might be in that line. There is no limit to the scope for advertising a programme.

A club should devise a constitution (the national body should be able to provide a facsimile of one). Find out about the conduct of meetings and annual general meetings. Officers should know their duties and the fixture secretary should have a procedure. It is mainly a job for one year working for the next year's fixtures in liaison with the national fixture list.

COMPETITIONS

Whether running club, local, county or national competitions, it is good to know the different methods and the one suitable for your needs. This depends on size of venue, restriction of numbers and other factors.

There are many advantages to being affiliated to the national body. One of the chief advantages is being insured and being able to enter national competitions.

CONDUCT OF PLAYERS

A club should from the beginning set out a code of ethics, for instance:

Use of equipment.
Punctuality.
Negative chat, such as how unfit you are and so on. Negative chat can lower the morale even more.
Etiquette on the piste.
Expenses.
Dress.
Captains of teams.

Fitness and training. If you are not fit, you should let the captain know. Better that than letting your team down.

Addressing officials.

Demonstration (controlling your emotions).

Tributes, i.e. three short cheers if a team or a handshake afterwards, if individuals.

Cleanliness.

Trophies, prizes and presentation.

Value of, caring of, record of, useful presents and presentation. Cash prizes could impair amateur status.

Physical training, as explained in Chapter 5, should be a must for every class. The power of the brain is affected by poor fitness so fencers should keep in good physical shape. Physical training types fall into two groups: before 18 years of age and between 18 and 40. Over 40 exercise is more gentle, similar to that of an 18 year old. Youngsters should be physically educated to realize the benefit and purpose of their training.

Training should be planned so that it is pleasurable and not boring. Exercises should include mental alertness and co-ordination and should include an element of challenge. Exercises can be done in pairs and threes. Variations in group formations breaks up the monotony of the weekly movement exercises.

Immediate training and discipline in looking after and storage of equipment will not only save money, but will also instil a discipline in looking after your own equipment.

JUDGING AND PRESIDING

In my opinion, the electric box has to some extent eliminated faulty presiding. Nowadays, many presidents will not preside without a box, so now we are getting presidents

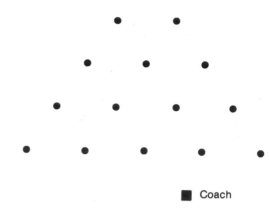

■ Coach

Figs 166 and 167   Different patterns for organizing groups during training.

■ Coach

Fig 167

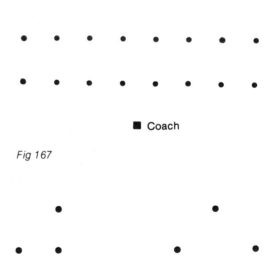

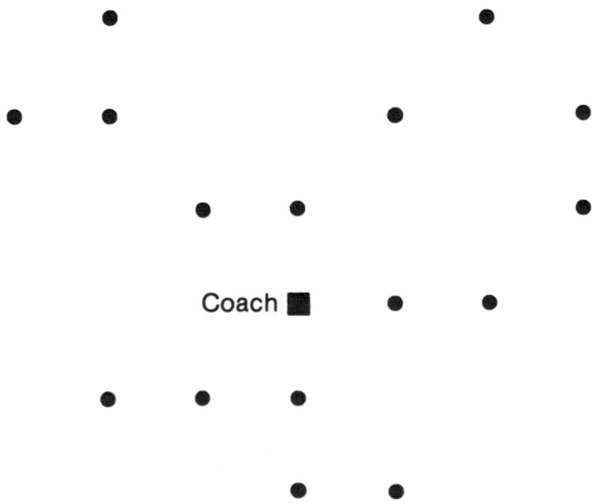

Coach ■

Fig 168   Instead of a regular formation, pupils are working in their own area.

who let the box decide the hits, especially where the remise comes before the direct riposte. If two lights come up, 'simultaneous attacks' is the cry. One other danger is where a president favours a certain fencer. Although there are rules governing this, organizers can do little or nothing about it.

As my pupils practise in pools, they soon get to know about hits and also what an attack and parry riposte is, from presiding and learning the right of way. The person in charge is the president and pupils should be aware of his authority, even to the extent that he can have any coach or spectator removed for ungentlemanly conduct. The president has six assistants: four judges, each of whom stands one metre behind either side of the fencer; one scorekeeper; and one timekeeper.

The president ensures that the fencers salute correctly and do not just wave the sword around like a wand. The president and the judges acknowledge the salute by bowing at the waist (not too low). The president then states 'On guard; are you ready? Play'. He does not have to wait for a reply — it is up to the fencer to say whether he is ready or not. (There is a rule against wasting time.)

As soon as the judges, who move up and down with the fencers, see a hit they must put their hands up clearly when 'Halt' is called by the president. They answer either 'Yes', 'Yes, off', 'No', 'Abstain'. 'Yes' is a good hit with the point with enough penetration to draw blood. 'Yes, off' is a hit anywhere except the trunk of the body and the bib of the mask. 'No' is a hit that is not flat or plaqué. 'Abstain' means that the judge has seen a hit, but is not sure if it is either 'Yes' or 'Yes, off'. A president has the power of one and a half votes and a judge one. Two judges can overrule the opinions of a president; if both judges disagree, a president can form an opinion either for or against. A president

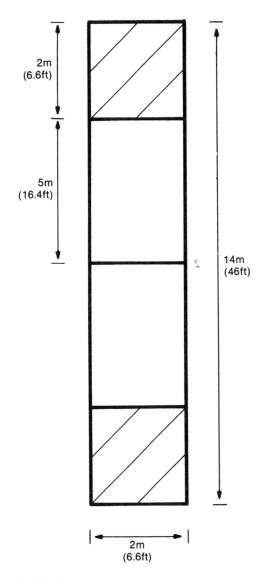

Fig 169   The piste.

should keep quiet if his opinion would not alter the decision. The president alone decides who has the right of way and analyses the order of movement. Neither the fencers nor the judges may question the president's analysis. The president should

Club Organization

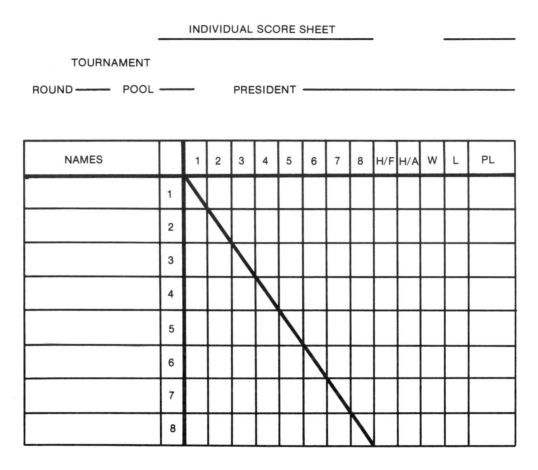

INDIVIDUAL SCORE SHEET

TOURNAMENT

ROUND ——— POOL ——— PRESIDENT ———————————

NAMES		1	2	3	4	5	6	7	8	H/F	H/A	W	L	PL
	1													
	2													
	3													
	4													
	5													
	6													
	7													
	8													

Fig 170   The score sheet shows Collingham (1) vs Hunt (4). To fill in the number of hits for Collingham, go along line 1 until you meet colum 4; for Hunt do the reverse. Call out the score after each hit. The person who scores five hits wins – in this case it is Collingham. As a practice exercise, fill in the score for player 3 vs player 5 if player 3 won 5 hits to 1.

gather the votes in by asking the furthest judge, then the nearest judge. Judges should not look at each other. A less experienced judge often looks at the other judge but should just trust in his own judgement.

A fencer cannot argue with a president's decision, unless it contradicts with regulations, for example, if both judges say 'Yes', the president cannot say 'No'.

Fencing with the electric box does away in a sense with the use of judges, but the box can only show hits; it does not know the rules, so when the president sees lights either side on at the same time, the president must decide who is awarded the hit. The lights on a box show white red and white green. If a white light precedes a coloured light on either side, no hit is awarded. A very useful exercise to improve judging and presiding, is to have a box and cover it. Have the fencers wired up; choose a president and four judges. When the president hears the buzzer, the bout is stopped, the judges are asked and give an opinion. The president also gives an opinion, then the cover is removed. At the beginning there are surprising results. With practice accuracy improves, but it does show human error.

The timekeeper measures the time of a fight. He starts the clock when the president says 'Play' and stops it when the president says 'Halt'. A few seconds before the one-minute warning, the timekeeper attracts the president's attention who calls 'Halt' and tells the fencers they have one minute left for fencing. At the end of time, the timekeeper calls out 'Halt'.

The scorer keeps the score and calls the names of the next competitors to be ready. After each hit, he calls out the score. At the end of the pool, he adds up the results and gets the president to sign the score sheet.

8 The Coach

Methods have changed since I started coaching, and will do so again. The whole object of fencing is to get into combat and win, and win well, but whether a fencer wins or loses, coaches should listen to their pupils to get feedback. For instance:

Ability 'I felt good. My attacks were coming off well.'
Effort 'If I had tried harder, I would have beaten him.'
Difficulty 'That was easy; he was only a beginner' or 'He was left-handed.'
Luck 'He was lucky; the president was on his side.'

Does this information coincide with the thoughts of the coach? Remember it is the learner who learns, and if he realizes his weaknesses, he can work on them. Does the coach make the pupil aware of where he is hitting on the target and not just going through the motions of hitting? In a similar way, a darts player has to be aware of the whole dart board and not just be able to throw treble 20s; he must also be adept at throwing double 1s.

The coach should make the pupil aware of what is a good movement, i.e. one that combines skill, power, strength, timing and distance. He should be made aware of whether one movement is better than the other, then try to repeat that movement time and time again. Once the practice stage has improved, then comes the automatic stage. The fencer does not have to think about his skill anymore. The only time that the fencer becomes aware of failure is either when he is hit or when he misses with an attack or riposte. The good fencer has time to think about technique and tactics as they proceed with the merest prompting on the part of the opponent. It is a difficult task to coach out errors that have become automatic responses. It is another reason why I do not agree with loose play, for it is difficult to iron out bad habits.

FEEDBACK AND SELF-EVALUATION

A good coach works hard to present information in the appropriate way to suit all pupils. The coach should analyse his performance and let others check on his performance. I once had useful information from a psychologist who knew nothing about fencing, but who was able to correct me on my presentation and dialogue. A coach who is prepared to learn from his pupils gets the fencer to feed back to the coach the feeling of his performance in a fight.

The coach should not try and get his pupil to assimilate too many points at one time, nor should he try to correct too many faults at one time. It is like a teacher marking an essay and correcting all the faults until it seems to be more faults than good points. The coach should concentrate on one aspect at a time and try to deal with it. For example, too many fencers return to guard incorrectly. The coach and pupil should concentrate on this one point, and when that has been corrected another fault can be taken for correction.

The coach's job can be both rewarding and frustrating. It is particularly frustrating for a coach when his pupils show a lack of commitment. Another problem is getting the pupil to realize his failings. The coach can seek the help of others to pin-point the same fault in a pupil; if enough people notice the same fault, the pupil can then re-examine his own performance and seek improvement.

Some problems are caused when communication breaks down, resulting in conflict. For instance, a fencer is selected for a team and the coach is the last to know. Administrators and coaches must work together.

Coaching beginners involves other responsibilities. For instance, parents need to know what the season holds in store for their children so as to reduce confusion of what to expect. To avoid misunderstanding, letters should be signed and returned by the parent.

There is talk of pupils' burn out, but coaches also burn out, both physically and mentally. A lot of people expect a great deal of a coach, but coaches also need motivation to boost their confidence. Coaches should do three things: decide what is best for their programmes and their fencers; devise a syllabus to suit the overall ability of their fencers; and, lastly, sort out priorities. They should also look at their own ability and only coach as far as their own ability allows them.

Fencers like a controlled, regulated programme, but it is also important that there is life in the syllabus. This can be done by keeping practices at a fast steady pace. If pupils do not grasp the practice, introduce a new idea with the same goals; there are several ways of teaching the simple parry — all with the same result. Coaches should be enthusiastic; share a spirited attitude with the fencers; include competitive skills, one to one and group to group.

To preserve his freshness and enthusiasm, a coach must:

Establish programmes.
Establish goals.
Organize practices.
Make sure results are known.
Allow for disappointments — be prepared to deal with them.
Make it fun to be part of a team or club.
Be encouraged to work with senior coaches to be able to keep up with the latest methods of coaching and to be able to attract good fencers.
Develop a hobby outside coaching.
Make time to relax.
Have a sense of humour.

A coach must sum up his pupils' abilities. A coach cannot make all his pupils champions.

A coach should give guidelines and find out what the pupil wants from the beginning. He should establish a work schedule throughout the season and have fencers do a progress chart with a goal for each week and each month. This will also help towards pin-pointing improvement.

PSYCHOLOGY OF FENCING

When a fencer comes into a room, what do we know of the person? We see only the exterior. But what makes them 'tick'? As coaches, we should also study the psychology of a pupil. In Russia and in some sports in America, a study is made of each pupil before they are taken on as students or competitors. Many a person has failed at the moment of crisis. One has heard of athletes creating world records to a stop-watch, but failing in the Olympics because their coaches have failed to recognize the pupil's weaknesses. Not only must the coach be able to recognize the weaknesses but he must also be able to cure them. Any doctor who is not a specialist in any particular field must pass his patient on to someone who is, in the event of his patient needing specialist treatment. The same pattern should be followed by the coach. He can diagnose a fault or symptom and be unable to cure it, so other opinions should be sought.

A beginner coach should have his own philosophy and understand the philosophy of the club. Before changing entirely this philosophy of the club, the coach must find out the general feeling before he goes headlong into any conflict. A coach should identify valuable information by observation of current practices, reading, clinics, workshops, media and films. Finally, a coach might have to revise *his* philosophy!

Coaches should have a master plan. This will depend upon the pupils he has. There should be scope and sequence and organization ideas.

What do we mean by scope or coaching knowledge? Besides rules, regulations, principles and skills, are added other disciplines: physiology, psychology, sociology, etc. One might not have to teach it, but an understanding of it will greatly enrich the other skills that are already possessed. The coach must know what he should be looking for; this will lead to critical observation at competitions and practice. He also needs to know why. Video has become an important means of analysing faults, but this must be carefully planned in use; otherwise it can be a waste of time.

Personal Qualities of the Coach

Coaching is a personalized way of imparting knowledge. No two coaches are alike. A style that suits one does not necessarily suit another, but pupils will follow certain traits of a coach as that is the only guide-line they can follow. I think it is unwise for any beginner or person in his early training to have more than one coach, as they are not experienced enough to adjust their knowledge and decide which is best, leading to confusion and in the end deterioration of standard.

It is often the case that students go to other coaches as they believe, or have been told to believe, that they can do better, and before long they have slipped down in the ratings and finally get frustrated and give up.

Successful coaches have other traits regardless of style: understanding, ability to motivate, tolerance and a sense of humour.

It is the responsibility of the coach to develop the maximum potential and ability in each pupil and the ways in which he can do this are numerous. I am afraid some coaches are motivated by money first and do not do their job as coaches. Learning to fence well is a slow process and sometimes the fencer has not the patience. As fencers get more experienced, the coach has to put a greater pressure on the pupil. This extra pressure can sometimes be too much for the pupil. The coach has to realize that there are numerous other outside influences to distract a person.

When teaching a subject, the presentation of the material should be clear, concise and simple, especially in fencing as it is a language on its own, and also very technical. Lack of progress or improvement can be blamed on making instructions too complex or too many at one time. I do not advocate the old system of doing instructions by numbers, but I feel there has been too much of a swing the other way. The coach educates pupils and should encourage them to play with thought and understanding and to ask questions.

The coach may have the responsibility of working with an assistant who should be helped in developing his own skill and coaching style and the role when instructing. The coach as the person in charge will be responsible for discipline both on and off the piste. A person with discipline will also be well disciplined when fencing. A coach needs to be an organizer and have an orderly and methodical approach, whether it be in administration, teaching aids, charts or in the practical aspects of the sport.

The coach must also fill the role of counsellor. This is a very important part of a coach's duties, especially with young fencers. As the Russians state, you have to know everything about your pupil and be ready to lend a sympathetic ear and solve even personal problems. Some coaches say they even want to know if their pupils cough! A pupil who is tense and worried will not perform well.

Creating Attitudes

The coach has to build on or create attitudes in pupils in order for them to become better fencers. Desire is a very important thing to create in a pupil. The coach can motivate a desire to learn, to improve, to compete and to win. I still believe in the maxim 'You can take a horse to water but you cannot make it drink'. You must analyse desire: how strong is it? How long does the desire keep up and if it fails, what are the reasons?

The Coach's Responsibilities

The chief one is to develop and maximize potential and ability within each pupil. Teacher presentation of material should be clear, precise and concise. Lack of improvement can often be blamed on too many complex instructions at any one time.

The coach should get his pupils to fence with understanding and not be afraid to ask questions.

The coach is also responsible for training the captain in his duties. A captain is usually selected according to experience. The captain and coach work together and should represent the ideal model in terms of example. The club should be welded together in an harmonious atmosphere.

The coach should have sufficient technical knowledge to meet the requirements of any particular group being coached.

These comments are only scratching the surface but they are meant to stimulate leaders and coaches to further investigation and self-analysis in their coaching.

9 Training

PROCEDURE FOR TRAINING CAMP PROGRAMME

The first day arrives and everybody is nervous. The organizers are hoping it will be successful. The pupils are wondering what is in store. It is therefore important that the initial organization is sound. If you start a course with underlying grumbles, it carries on to the end.

First, coaches must be sure to be there to greet everyone. There might be parents or even adult fencers asking questions. Supervise billeting. Instil tidiness from the beginning. Introduce yourself and the team. Get the pupils introduced. Tell them the rules and regulations, the treating of other people's property. Thoughtfulness to others, at meal times and at night. A programme should be outlined and displayed.

Sessions should not be longer than an hour and a half without refreshments. Sessions should be demanding so there is no time for talking and time wasting.

Evenings should be organized and have various activities. Either team fencing or even an activity not connected with fencing at all. There could be a quiet hour after the evening meal; films or videos could be shown; small games, such as cards, monopoly, chess, draughts can be made available. If the sessions have been hard enough, people will want to turn in early.

Break a week up by having a half-day visit to somewhere not necessarily connected with fencing. It is also useful to have a visitor, as it will be a different face (not the same old one each day). In the evening, there could be a lecture on some aspect of fencing, such as psychology or physiology.

The organizer should know where to obtain a doctor, first aid equipment, fire equipment and he should know the procedure in case of fire. The organizer should also be on hand to answer any queries and if necessary deal with them as soon as it is practical. He must supervise meals and duties. If there are few problems it will make for a happy course.

FENCING TRAINING SEQUENCES

1. Lunging. Throwing the point. Execution. A lunging B with a mask on in front and to the side ready to catch foil.
Points to notice The foil should go straight as an arrow.
2. Riposting distance. On guard. A disengages, B parry quartes. A should hit B as A has a period of fencing time in hand. This is good for concentration and fingers.
Points to notice A must not extend arm first; B must not extend arm first, B must not pull back arm in parry of quarte.
3. Lunging. Parry quarte late.
Points to notice The timing of the parry. Too early it can be deceived; too late you will be hit.
4(a) A Lunges. B counters in sixte.
Points to notice The sound of the parry. It should be a sharp bang, not a scrape.
(b) Follow lunge with a double. *Note*: First movement by A must threaten target of B.

Points to notice The lunge should follow in one line pushing hard on the last movement.

5.   Riposting distance. A disengages. B counters in quarte.

Points to notice As in No. 2

6.   Return beats: first with use of thumb and index finger; then with all the fingers on the handle.

Points to notice The beat should be that of a clock — a regular tick-tock.

(b)   B then deceives blade of A.

(c)   A then does counter of quarte of B's deception. Useful for concentration, feeling of blade and finger play. Try to deceive on eighth counter or not more than twelfth.

7.   A has arm extended; B parry quarte ripostes high or low.

Points to notice Pronation when hitting to flank. Supination when hitting to stomach. Have legs lower when riposting low.

8.   Successive parries start with one blade movement and work up a sequence.

counter—sixte
counter—sixte—counter—sixte
counter—sixte—counter—sixte—parry
  quarte
counter—sixte—counter—sixte—parry
  quarte—counter quarte and so on.

9.   Present blade for accurate timing; then A presents blade and attacks with B riposting. Spectators observe what has been done, then act as B. For example, A disengages parry quarte on lunge. B parrys in quarte and indirect riposte.

10.   Coulé, disengage; lunge keeping contact with the blade until the last moment, then disengage.

11.   Scrub fencing. Up to 21

Example: 5 points for simple attack
            3 points indirect riposte and
              counter riposte
            2 points compound attack
            2 points redoublement

WORK ON A BEAM

If at your fencing club there is a gymnastic beam, one that stands about three feet off the floor and is four inches wide, try these exercises:

1.   Walk along the beam to gain confidence, eyes looking ahead, partner walking on floor in case pupil overbalances.

2.   Walk backwards.

3.   Advance along the beam, then dismount. Keep trying until you can advance as if you were following a line on the floor.

4.   Move backwards.

5.   Advance, with crossing of the feet, forward then backward.

6.   Next lunge. Then bring up rear foot, and lunge again.

7.   Next do a balestra forward and a balestra backward.

8.   Combine these movements of breaking and gaining ground.

9.   Introduce mobility.

With conscientious practice, balance will vastly improve. One of my pupils can move on a beam as if he were on the floor.

LESSONS WITH CHALK

If you have a class without equipment or with a limited amount, try a few of the following exercises. Work in pairs. Mark the on guard position, then:

1.   Step forward, then step backward. Check position against marks.

2.   Vary the number of steps forward and backward, coming back to the same position.

3.   The lunge. Mark the on guard position,

then lunge, then return to guard, checking the position.

4. Vary the gaining and breaking ground movements with the lunge.

The Lunge

1. Mark the limit of the lunge.
2. Do a step with the front foot, and mark.
3. Do two steps, lunge and mark.
4. Do a single lunge: you should find that you are lunging further than your initial first mark.

Target Practice

Foils Only

Chalk an eye-level mark on the wall, then draw a target or a face, and award points for various positions. Allow so many attempts, for instance, five or ten, then add the total. Do it first at riposting distance, then advance at riposting distance, then lunging distance, then step forward and lunge, then balestra lunge, and any other combinations for the experienced. If in pairs, make it competitive.

Circular Parry

When doing a circular parry, the blade should describe a full circle. Get pupils to draw a circle on the wall or floor with the point in the chalk.

Amazing results will show that rarely is there a complete circle. Show and explain the faults that they draw, for instance:

Point finishes too low.
Point finishes too high.
Point goes round too far.
Point does not go round far enough.

COMPOUND MOVEMENTS

1. A advance lunge with straight thrust; return covering on guard.
   B riposte with straight thrust.
2. A press lunge. Return to guard.
   B riposte with disengage.
   A simple parry of quarte and direct riposte.
3. A in sixte on change of engagement to quarte.
   B disengage and lunge.
4. A beat on 'B' return of beat. Disengage and lunge.
   B counter sixte and riposte by disengage.
5. A flèche attack.
   B retire one pace and counter sixte and riposte.
6. A advance and lunge with disengagement.
   B parry quarte and riposte by cut over.
   A counter quarte and riposte.
7. A feint low.
   B parry octave.
   A lunge high.
   B parry quarte.
8. A feint low.
   B parry octave.
   A lunge high.
   B parry quarte and riposte by disengagement.
9. A envelope.
   B counter envelope.
10. A make absence of blade.
    B lunge low.
    A parry octave and riposte low.
11. A beat, lunge, high return to guard, beat and lunge low.
12. A advance lunge out of distance and beat, reprise.
13. A lunge with disengagement.

B parry quarte and riposte.
A stay on lunge and parry quarte and riposte by disengagement.
B counter quarte and riposte.
14. A advance with disengagement with lunge.
B retire with counter sixte and riposte.
15. A cut over.
B stop hit.
A parry septime and lunge high on A's return to guard.
16. A beat extend on B's envelopment.
A draw back arm.
B disengage.
A counter sixte and lunge.
17. A advance with feint of 1, 2.
B stop hits.
A on stop hit counter-times with parry riposte.
18. A feint low.
B parry octave and bind to quarte and riposte with disengagement.
A parry sixte.
B redoublement.
19. A advance with change of engagement.
B counter disengage.
A counter quarte.
B disengage and lunge.
A parry sixte.
B reprise with disengagement.
20. A feint low.
B parry octave.
A cut over in low line and lunge.
B parry septime.
21. A disengage.
B counter sixte.
A redoublement.
B step back.
A reprise of redoublement.

LOOSE PLAY

When I first started fencing, I learnt for six months before being allowed to fence. On a visit to Germany in the 1960s, the pupils told me that it was their first fight after two years' training and we beat them. It has now gone the other way: let them fight first; then try and train them afterwards. Pupils who are allowed to 'bash' around without prior training soon get bored, quite apart from getting poked and rapped across the knuckles. My lessons usually end in supervised pools and they also get the practice in presiding, judging and fencing etiquette. How the system works depends on time.

First, have seven fencers in a group of eight or nine; the extra ones are stand-bys. Two fencers first salute the president, who acknowledges by bowing the head; then the opposite judges, who also acknowledge; then the opponent. (In olden days they kissed the blade for good luck.) At the end of the fight, the president goes on to the piste and all the judges move round clockwise and the loser goes into the left-hand corner. The winner stays on until defeated.

Fencers will have two thoughts in mind. First, all they have been taught seems to fly out of the window as they face an opponent who wants to hit them, and they go all out to beat him. Second, they fence an experienced fencer and all they want to do is beat him. There are ways to improve this if you are not giving individual lessons. It can be used as a time for presiding and judging, and for learning the rules and regulations regarding the fight and the piste. It can also be used as a period for stopping and making pupils think of the most advantageous way of attacking or defending. For a change, sometimes you can deduct hits in timed bouts. For example, hits can be deducted for not saluting correctly, not

Fig 171   The salute. Ready position.

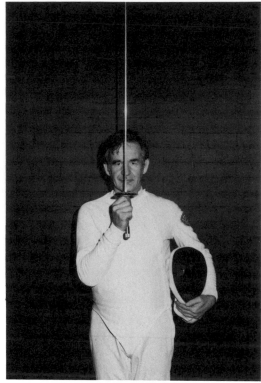

Fig 172   The salute. Finish position.

returning on guard correctly, lunging with a bent arm and so on.

If you do fence in pairs, salute each other first and then try to put into practice either the work you have done in groups or in individual lessons. In this period, results do not count so if you are hit, acknowledge by raising your hand. Off-targets annul any further good hits. If in doubt scrub it out. In practice sessions, people do wonderful lunges, but when in free play, they forget. Remember, lunging can be very successful and can keep you further away from your opponent. Use the length of the piste; many fencers only use half of it. Get your feet 'twinkling' using cadence. Probe out your opponent, making false attacks, or reactions on your preparations.

Some fencers attack at the outset before their opponents have time to settle down. When you have had some practice, have five hits, then change opponents. One common fault amongst experienced fencers is that they fight only experienced fencers, but they should remember that they were beginners once; also it is very useful to watch how a beginner attacks and how they defend. So analyse, then make the appropriate movement.

You must realize early on that fencing is not like that portrayed in films. For a start, there are no castle walls, only a gymnasium, and you must learn control and have patience, and this must be emphasized as much as the skills of movement. Do not rush.

Although successful at first, when you get to the second round, you will find it of no use against experienced fencers. Try and move your feet and use the entire length of the piste. Make false attacks to see their reactions. Fencers usually come in two types: ones that like to attack and those that like to defend. Therefore, attack the attacker and provoke the defender to attack. The élite fencer does both.

You should have been taught fencing from an engaged position or from an absence of blade position. If you find a fencer who wants to knock 'seven bells' out of your blade, keeping the arm in the same position, lower your blade. It is very disconcerting when there is no blade to attack. Make sure he does not get to judge your distance. If you find you are being hit, take a step back in order to have time to get in your parry. You will also notice that many attacks fail, which can be used to your advantage. Use a renewal. After being parried, disengage and hit, or if he ripostes lunge short, draw the riposte and counter riposte. Try and start off all your movements in offence with a straight arm, and practise using your fingers.

Finally, realize that practice makes perfect, then loose play will make for enjoyable fencing.

Competition

There are four types of competition, a local or junior competition, and a minor open competition, or high-class one. When a coach wishes to advise a pupil which sort of competition to enter he must first consider how the pupil has been coached technically

Fig 173 Competition in progress. Note the electric spools on the floor.

and psychologically. Personally, I prefer to enter a pupil in a high-class field so that my pupil, although likely to lose, will meet fencers doing movements he has been taught. Not only will he be faced with the awe and atmosphere of the meeting, he will meet people of high quality. My pupils have recognized the dignified atmosphere, the sportsmanship and chiefly been able to recognize a proper parry and riposte and correct lunging. One of my pupils was only ten when she entered the Senior Section Championships and scored two hits. At the age of eleven she defeated the Hamburg Ladies Champion in a match and went on to fence for the 'Rest of Britain'. Another boy, aged thirteen, at the Leamington Open gave an Australian Olympic fencer the fright of his life. By fencing in a high-quality competition, you can learn a great deal and if you do well you will find older fencers ready to give you advice and encouragement. The coach must prepare his pupil for losing though. I have seen too many children go off crying.

Appendices

I RULES AND REGULATIONS

The Rules can be purchased from the AFA and, as they often change, amendments can be purchased. Why does a competitor need to know the rules? Just recently two experienced fencers did not know that if you find your point not working immediately after your opponent has hit you, that hit has to be annulled, but only if you get the president to test it straight away before you come on guard again. In this case, it cost one person the fight: the hit in question was the last one. You are not allowed to bang it on the floor then give it to the president to test. If the president gets it to register, the hit remains good.

Some Rules to Note

There is now no warning line, but a line in a different colour across the piste 2 metres from the end. If both feet are off the end, it constitutes a hit against.

A card system has now been introduced. Yellow, red and black. The yellow card constitutes a warning valid for the bout, in some cases annulment of any hit scored by the fencer at fault, for instance, turning back on opponent. A red card and penalty hit is given for a second offence. If you commit another offence of a different nature, i.e. refusal to obey the president, you get an immediate red card. A black card means exclusion or expulsion. A spectator, trainer, or fencer not on piste also comes under this category. Deliberate brutality would mean exclusion; so does doping.

II FENCING AWARDS AND ASSOCIATIONS

The British Fencing Association

The Amateur Fencing Association (AFA) is the UK governing body responsible for the development of fencing from schools and clubs to the training of Olympic teams. It provides rules and regulations and it administers grants from the Sports Council. It assists handicapped fencers. As a member of the FIE it is insured against accidents.

The British Academy of Fencing

The British Academy of Fencing is concerned with the development of amateur coaches and professional standard of coaches.

National Coaching Awards

There are four levels at all three weapons:

Basic This introduces the different methods of teaching. The teaching of a range of strokes and movements to classes and individuals.

Intermediate This is the minimum qualification to instruct at evening classes or clubs. It covers the teaching and coaching of a wider range of strokes.

Advanced This covers a whole variety of

movements and strokes with tactical applications to more advanced individuals and classes. Introduction to elementary anatomy, psychology and physiology.

Diploma This is the highest coaching award and covers all aspects of training and coaching. It requires a more detailed study of fencing theory, together with anatomy, physiology and psychology.

Club Leaders Award

This is an award designed to acknowledge members who assist the coach in the club and also to encourage them to make the next step and take a basic award. Safety is of the prime importance for this award as is knowledge of the principles and use of the weapon. It teaches you how to officiate, how to supervise basic blade and body movements. It gives you a knowledge of organization at club, local and national level. For further details of this award, contact The Development Officer at the AFA (*see* Useful Addresses).

Further Reading

Evered, D.F., *Sabre Fencing*, (Duckworth, 1982).

Harris, Dorothy V. and Harris, Bette L., *Sports Psychology*, (Champaign, Illinois, 1984).

Manley, Albert, *Complete Fencing*, (Robert Hale, 1979).

Peterson, Lars, *Sports Injuries: Their Prevention and Treatment*, (Martin Dunitz, 1983).

Schuber, *Psychology from Start to Finish*, (Sports Book Publishers, Canada).

Simmonds, A.T. & Morton, E.D. *Start Fencing*, (Sportsman's Press, London, 1989).

Vass, Imre, *Épée Fencing*, 1976.

Winckles, H.A. and Weeks, Waltham, *Sports Organiser's Book*, 1957.

Two useful publications are:

Sabre View, for details contact:
Graham Walls,
7 Chandos Road East,
Finchley,
London N2 9AR

Athlete Ability – Anatomy of Winning,
for details contact:
Rolf Wished,
National Coaching Foundation,
4 College Close,
Beckett Park,
Leeds LS6 3QN.

Useful Addresses

AFA Headquarters
1 Baron's Gate
33–35 Rothschild Road
London W4 5HT
0181 742 3032

Leon Paul Equipment Company
Units 1 and 2 Cedar Way
Camley Street
London NW1 0JQ

M Fare (The Sword)
15 Rastell Avenue
London SW2 4XP
0171 261 8474

Coaches Club
Mrs H. Hammond
9 Beverley Close
Aston Bank
Redditch
R96 6DX

Northern Ireland AFA
Miss K. Lowry
40 Groomsport Road
Bangor
County Down
BT20 5LR

Marilyn Wheelband
49 Blenheim Gardens
Grove
Wantage
Oxfordshire OX12 0NP
01235 769978

Welsh AFA
Ms A. Charles
37 Lansdown Avenue East
Canton
Cardiff CF1 8BU
01222 371 844

Schools Fencing
Mr J. Ramsey
Tuedhuse
Hadleigh Road
Hotlen St Mary
Suffolk
01473 310101

Veteran Fencing
H. de Silva
6 Little Meddow
Andreas
Isle of Man
IM7 4HY
01624 880949

Scottish Fencing
C. Grahamshaw
40 Bogmoor Place
Glasgow
G51 4TQ
0141 445 1602

Channel Islands
Mrs P. Sauvarin
La Villette de Hau
St Martin's
Guernsey
01481 37923

Glossary

Absence of blade Fencers' weapons not in contact.

Engagement Blades in contact.

Manipulators Thumb and index finger.

Aids Other three fingers used to control the sword.

Attack The initial extension of the arm, designating the right of way.

Balestra A short jump forward followed by a lunge.

Barrage A fence-off between fencers who have tied in bouts win.

Beat A sharp, crisp blow on the opponent's blade, either deflecting or creating a reaction.

Bent-Arm Attack An arm not extending when attacking. It is subject to a counter attack which if arriving before the attack in one period of fencing time would be valid.

Bind Taking of the blade diagonally across the target.

Bout A fight between two fencers.

Breaking ground Forward or backward movement.

Broken time A pause between two movements.

Cadence Rhythm of a movement.

Ceding parry Yielding to a taking of the blade.

Change beat A beat after the change of engagement.

Change of line High to low and inside to outside and vice versa.

Circular or counter parry A movement of the blade performed by the fingers returning to the original point of engagement.

Close quarters Able to engage still in a phrase.

Closing the line Blocking an opponent's attack.

Compound attack An attack comprising of two or more blade movements, each previous movement being a feint.

Compound riposte A riposte comprised of one or more feints.

Coquille The guard of either foil or épée.

Corps-à-corps Body contact which prohibits further play.

Coulé A straight thrust down an opponent's blade.

Counter-attack Stop hit or stop hit with opposition. This should not be encouraged with beginners.

Counter riposte Offensive action after successfully parrying the attack.

Counter-time Even action made by an attacker against the opponent's counter attack.

Coupé Cut over, i.e. a disengagement over the blade.

Covered Action taken to close a line from an attacker.

Croisé Forte to foible and taking the blade down by lowering wrist and forearm.

Deceive To evade an action by an opponent.

Dérobement Evasion of an attack on the blade of the defender.

Detachment parry A crisp parry which deflects but leaves the blade immediately after contact.

Development The lunge.

Direct thrust A simple direct attack in the same line of engagement.

Director Also known as the president who supervises the bout and awards hits.

Glossary

Disengage A blade movement that passes under an opponent's blade into a different line.

Double A compound attack that deceives a circular or counter parry.

En finalé A parry at the last moment.

Envelopment Taking the opponent's blade in a circular movement to the original line of engagement done on an opponent's straight arm.

Épée Advanced form of duelling weapon.

False attack An attack to test out the reaction of the opponent.

Feint A movement to deceive.

Fencing measure The practical distance between two opponents so that when on the lunge they can hit each other.

Fencing time Time taken to execute any action of the blade or body or combination of both.

Finger play Dexterity of the fingers and complete relaxation when making blade movements.

Flèche A running attack from out of distance.

Foible The weakest part of the blade used for beating.

Foil Type of weapon.

Forte The strongest part of the blade used for parrying.

Froissement A strong attack down the opponent's blade, deflecting it.

Gaining ground The advance.

Ground judges Two judges, one at each end, to determine floor hits.

High lines Target area above the level of the guard.

Hit An offensive action where the point in a forward motion hits the opponent with enough penetration to draw blood. A hit can be off or on target.

Immediate Usually relating to the riposte.

Indirect A simple blade movement finishing in the opposite line to the engagement.

In line A position where the sword-arm is extended and threatening the target.

In quatata A defensive counter-attack where the body is removed by a side-step from the incoming blade. This needs precise timing.

Inside lines The lines either low or high on the sixte side.

Insufficient parry Does not deflect the oncoming blade.

Invitation The opening of a line to encourage an attack.

Jury President and judges officiating at a match.

La belle Deciding touch when both people are tied.

Lateral parry Movement of the arm laterally to deflect the opponent's blade.

Lunge The forward projection of the body in order to hit your opponent.

One-two A compound attack consisting of two disengages on opponent's lateral parry.

Opposition A holding of opponent's blade preventing an attack or riposte.

Outside lines The high and low target areas opposite to the sword-arm.

Parry A defensive movement of application of the forte to opponent's foible, with the characteristic of deflection.

Passa ta sotto An offensive counter-attack which displaces the body by lowering it under the oncoming blade, executed at the same time with a straight arm.

Phrase The passing of movements back and forwards until someone is hit, which is determined by the president.

Point in line The arm is extended with the point threatening the target.

Pool A number of fencers grouped together to fence each other; the resulting winners qualify for the next round.

Preparation of attack Attacks on the blade — beat, change beat, pressure — froissement.

Gaining and breaking ground.
Step forward and backward.
Takings of the blade.
Bind, croisé, envelopment.

Prise de fer *see* taking of the blade.

Pronation Sword-hand position with knuckles facing up.

Redoublement Renewal of an attack while still on the lunge, either one or more blade movements.

Remise A renewal of an attack while on the lunge by replacing the point without any further action of the blade, body or combination of both.

Reprise A renewal of an attack preceded by a return to guard either forward or backward.

Right of way A convention of foil and sabre fencing. It is the attack characterized by an extending arm threatening the valid target. To gain the right of way from the attacker, the blade must be parried or evaded.

Riposte The offensive action taken by a defender after successfully parrying the attack.

Simple riposte A riposte of one blade movement either direct or indirect.

Simultaneous action Actions performed simultaneously by fencers, mainly conceived when two fencers are close together and are redoubling.

Stop hit Counter-attack.

Stop in time Counter-attack.

Stop with opposition Counter-attack.

Straight thrust Direct attack.

Supination Hand position with fingers up.

Taking the blade (Prise de fer.) The act of taking a blade on an extended arm.

Trompement A deception performed by the attacker.

FRENCH TERMS

Fencing today is chiefly related to the French school and so many of the terms used are French. Since you will often hear presidents presiding in French, it is helpful to be familiar with some of the more frequently used terms.

Allez Fench

Advertissement Warning

Après la parade After the parry

Arrêtez Halt

À droite For the right

À gauche For the left

À la coquille On the guard

Annulé Hit annulled

Attaque (l') The attack

Au bras On the arm

Au masque On the mask

Bon Good

Coup d'arrêt Stop thrust

Coup double Double hit

Contretemps Counter-time

Dégagez Disengage

En marche Advance lunge

Fleuret (le) Foil

Halte Halt

Liemente Bind

Mal paré Insufficient parry

Mesure Distance

Paré Parry

Pas de touche No touch

Pas valable Off target

Prèt Ready

Piste (la) The strip

Remise (la) Remise

Rien Nothing

Riposte (la) Riposte

Touché Hit

Trop bas Too low

Index